THE

STUDENT

LOOKS AT HIS

TEACHER

The Student Looks
at His Teacher

An inquiry into the implications of
student ratings at the college level.

✠
✠   ✠
✠

by JOHN W. RILEY, JR., BRYCE F. RYAN,
& MARCIA LIFSHITZ

1950
RUTGERS UNIVERSITY PRESS
NEW BRUNSWICK, NEW JERSEY

FOREWORD

THE American college professor, as a professional practitioner, stands in a unique relationship to the recipient of his service: only in most extreme cases is student judgment a factor seriously affecting the status, growth or retardation of an academic career. That student judgment exists there is no doubt, but by and large the professor is sheltered both situationally and psychologically from its influence. The very vagueness of definition of the goals or values in higher education precludes the formation of standards of judgment. Moreover, those most eager to judge, the very ones having direct access to the professor's wares—the students—are all too often deemed, *ipso facto*, incapable of competent evaluation. Thus, the professor has in a measure achieved a closed system of protective devices built upon the isolation of the classroom, disunity over educational goals, and the fact that the practice of the profession is upon a clientele alleged to be incapable of proper judgment.

It is the contention of this book that the student's construct of "good teaching" is closely relevant to the effectiveness of a teacher in reaching the student. Student judgment, however immature and however biased it often is, can be utilized to clarify central points and potential areas of tension between student and teacher.

The students' concepts of ideal and actual instruction, too long generally disregarded, should be faced and dealt with daily. While isolation from them may offer a seeming psychological security, maximum effectiveness can be achieved only through their critical recognition.

During recent years interest in the teacher at the college level has brought forth many books, articles and cryptic comments, many of them dealing with this phase of the subject. In some cases feeling has run high, as in Franz Schneider's *More Than An Academic Question,* which calls not only for the distribution of student-faculty reaction sheets on every campus, but also for a new type of dean to administer and utilize the results. Somewhat more philosophical in tone is Jacques Barzun's *Teacher in America,* which came close to the best-seller list by virtue of the pregnancy of its insight into the currently neglected profession. But whatever point of view recent observations adopt in their quest for light upon the dilemma of the teacher, they all point unmistakably to the obvious fact that teaching is a two-way process. And it is to this aspect of a large question that this volume is addressed.

In attempting to formulate the elements in this two-way process and to point out the need for further study of it, we have ourselves done some first hand research on the campus of Brooklyn College, under the aegis of President Harry Gideonse and with funds provided by the Carnegie Corporation of New York. We have lived through the experience of formulating, conducting and assessing a program of student evaluation on a single campus, and we shall report on both our techniques and our findings. But it is not our contention that these results constitute a model, or that they be interpreted as necessarily the best procedure. In fact, their validity and their applicability for other academic situations are considerations which bear only slightly upon our purpose. We propose simply to look at student ratings from the point of view of the larger issues. We are seeking perspective, and in this search we shall find it convenient to use much of our specific experience as a springboard. Nevertheless, the specific shortcomings and limitations of this particular experience are irrelevant to our thesis.

Perhaps not surprising is the history of opposition to the student ratings of college instructors, when the purpose of the rating was "to furnish 'evidence' to the President on the basis of which they (the instructors) may be reprimanded or dismissed." [1] Against this background, students have been accused of incompetence and lack of objectivity in their judgments. On the other hand, Dr. Cole in *The Background for College Teaching,* gives an excellent review of the experience with student rating scales. She concludes that the rating scale "has come to stay," that it has been shown to possess very high reliability and validity, and that students, after all, "are the only people who can or should rate a teacher."

Whatever the final decision on this question, it should be emphasized that the individual ratings of this investigation were never intended for the use of the college administrators. The reports on student ratings of individual instructors were held in strictest confidence. Their purpose was to acquaint the teacher with the student's reaction to his teaching, and to encourage him to re-evaluate his own teaching. To achieve the maximum constructive effects from this process, the instructor was also provided with an over-all analysis of the entire faculty positions and factors influencing student judgment.

A second departure from the usual student reaction study was the construction of a standard against which to measure student satisfaction with faculty achievement. Thus we have not only gathered the actual ratings of instructors but we have attempted to set up a yardstick whereby these ratings could be viewed against an "ideal."

A major objective of our work however, has been to go beyond the mere preparation of individual reports to an over-all analysis of the sum of these evaluations, also emphasizing their

---

1. Joel H. Hildebrand, "On Grading Without Judgment," AAUP Bulletin, Winter, 1945, p. 639.

relationships to student expectations. In this analytical approach we have been concerned with the necessity of learning more regarding the factors lying behind students' attitudes toward college instruction, as well as the extent to which background characteristics of both student and teacher influence the students' actual evaluations.

In this entire discussion we are writing for the academic man, be he the practicing teacher, the administrator, the serious student, or the literate layman. Such an audience is a broad one, for education, like freedom, is rapidly becoming "everybody's job." We present neither a technical handbook nor a philosophy of education, but rather an empirical and theoretical analysis of one aspect of the relationship between teacher and student. From this point of view, our effort may be construed as a sociological inquiry, for it was as "visiting" sociologists that we were called to the campus of Brooklyn College to analyze the problem and undertake a piece of research.

The volume is arranged in four parts. Part I describes the role of the professor, and discusses the nature of student-teacher relationships. Part II reviews the theory and practice of student evaluations and outlines their application on one campus. Part III presents the empirical findings of the study in terms of both student expectations and the actual ratings. Part IV shows how the teachers themselves reacted to the student evaluations, how such results may be translated into better teaching, and something of the research that yet needs to be done.

Although it would be impossible to make adequate acknowledgment to all the persons who contributed to this effort, special recognition must be accorded to some. In the first place, we should like to acknowledge our great debt to Professor H. H. Remmers of Purdue University, for it is his pioneering and continuing work in this field which has permitted others to make their contributions. At Brooklyn College, President Gideonse saw to it that the project was implemented, Professor Belle Zeller served as chairman of the faculty committee, and Bernard Neugeboren as chairman of the student committee, but special thanks are due to Dean Gaede and to Mr. Goodhartz of his office for their untiring efforts and consistent faith in the idea. To Drs. Raymond Franzen and Hans Zeisel acknowledgment is made for constructive statistical advice, and to Matilda White Riley for critical help and encouragement all along the line. Without her frequent expert advice we should have floundered often. We are also grateful to Professor Daniel Katz for his reading of the manuscript and the helpful comments and suggestions which he made. And finally to various members of their own staff, especially Frank Cantwell, Katherine Ruttiger, Melissa Nulton, Harriet Kipps, Renate Kerns, and Goldie Scarr, the authors are indebted. The task of ordering and processing the materials spawned from nearly forty thousand IBM punch cards was never an easy one. To the Research Council of Rutgers University thanks are due for supplementing the funds available for the present study. Without this assistance, it is doubtful whether the research could have been carried through to publication.

Finally, it can only be hoped that the work in some small part justifies the confidence placed in it by the Carnegie Corporation of New York. While the study was made possible by funds granted by them, the Corporation, of course, is in no way to be regarded as the sponsor of any of the views or findings herein presented. At this point the authors assume full responsibility.

JOHN W. RILEY, JR.
BRYCE F. RYAN
MARCIA LIFSHITZ

New Brunswick, N. J.
September, 1950

Contents

THE

STUDENT

LOOKS AT HIS

TEACHER

1

THE ROLE OF THE PROFESSOR

THE purposes and ends of higher education are in flux, and the classroom reflects the confusion of change. Student bodies have been recomposed. New secular motives, a new diversity of interests, wide ranges in abilities, great disparity in backgrounds, all crowd the classroom. For the professor to take shelter in his citadel of learning is almost to accept defeat. The learned professor venerated solely for his knowledge is largely a phenomenon of the past. The man of learning must meet his public; he must fulfill his obligations. And he must do so in a period when the nature of those obligations was never more obscure and where the complexities to which he must react effectively were never so great.

What manner of man is emerging? What roles must he play in the process? From what quarters do the pressures upon him rise?

The "average" college teacher is a composite figure. He may be a struggling graduate assistant or an eminent authority on matters of obscure scientific import. He may visualize himself as a teacher, with students at the core of his life; or he may accept instructional duties as a minor and possibly disagreeable handicap to his scientific and academic career. The academic life may be pursued as a strenuous intellectual career; or it may mean lolling in the sinecure of permanent tenure and small ease. Whatever may be the precise distribution of his time in teaching, college administration, community service and research, and whatever his status within the college community, it is certain that for few purposes can the college professor be categorized as a "type." However, as a teacher in the American pattern of higher education he must, consciously or unconsciously, conform with some degree of success to a series of roles.

The roles which the professor enacts arise both from the nature of instructional processes per se and from the unique definition and ideology of higher education in America. But as a teacher in our society the professor's career focuses on the classroom situation. In his instructional role he functions mainly through direct personal contact with students who meet with him under almost rigidly defined circumstances. And however the goals of his efforts may be defined, his "success" can be directly measured only through those students themselves and their works. Whatever the basis for "competence ratings" extant in American colleges, the evidence of instructional competence whether visible or not lies in the students as surely as the test of the physician lies ultimately in the patient.

Of all the professional careers, teaching, if not the most difficult of them, is surely the most difficult to evaluate. It is a process surrounded with the greatest confusions as to its ends, its arts and its techniques. Only in the most generalized terms can one find agreement upon the goals of classroom instruction, and even then we must be prepared to recognize that the nature of some courses will make the agreement all but meaningless. There is no standardized end toward which the professor works against which his efforts may be clearly weighed, no physician's concept of "normal health," no logical or pragmatic goal as for the jurist. The professor may spend a lifetime of professing with only a vague awareness as to the ends he has pursued—other than the imparting of substantive knowledge.

No one would argue today that the goal and purpose of the

teaching process is simply the transmission of data from the mind of a learned professor into the mind of an untutored copy-cat. The direct end of substantive instruction is, on the college level at least, quite meaningless apart from the concomitant objectives found in inculcating certain attitudes. These may be attitudes toward the subject matter at hand, toward knowledge itself, toward the ends for which knowledge is sought or even self attitudes by the recipient of knowledge. Some may even look upon the professor's classroom role as quite divorced from "knowledge," his function lying rather in the area of "inspiration," of "stimulus to creative achievement." The professor's role, as defined in current thinking, encompasses all of these functions and usually they are permitted to lie in this vague, ill defined and unrelated state. One of society's most revered institutions is beset with confusion.

Yet perhaps one thing is clear. The role of the professor is not simply that of a learned man. He is a learned man who can transmit his learning. Beyond that he is a learned man who must do more than transmit; he must stimulate, inspire, and instill values. These may be but slightly related to the fact that he is the master of his science. And if the fulfillment of the professorial role in respect to certain substantive ends can be measured by systematic and direct checks and the techniques of their attainment objectified, other and perhaps more basic ends defy such measurement. As Barzun provocatively points out, "You know by instinct that it is impossible to teach democracy or citizenship or a happy married life. I do not say that these virtues and benefits are not somehow connected with good teaching. They are, but they occur as by-products. They come not from a course but from a teacher; not from a curriculum, but from a human soul." [1]

Few parents, few educators, and few academicians would today assert that the professor's function has meaning in isolation from these nonobjectified, nontechnical ends. Professing is somewhat different and considerably more than the application of data to more or less absorptive human sponges. It is in just this area, this "over and beyond area," this "area of most vital significance" that the professor's role is obscured in a barrage of shibboleths, clichés and hopes built of pious egotism.

However rigorous a system of instruction may be, and how much singleness of purpose a teacher may possess, the classroom situation is not composed simply of learners and expositor. The classroom relationship is of total personalities focused upon a particular framework of study. Although modern specialization may obscure this fact, the "teacher" is not an abstraction of a personality, he is a whole personality in a particular focus. Whatever the teacher's store of pedagogical techniques and scientific learning, these elements provide only a share of his classroom performance. The teacher as a human being is a vital element even in the simple purveying of data, let alone the more subtle goals implicit in the instructional role. Quite accurately, Dean Cross of Yale recognized this in disavowing a particular questionnaire for "rating" teachers in his institution:

As yet we do not know with any degree of positiveness, what combinations of qualities make the successful teacher. There are doubtless various combinations. Of my own best teachers in school and in college one man was rather irritable; one was timid and shy; he limped and walked with a stick; another was sarcastic with an amusing streak of humor in his sarcasm; another disguised his seriousness under a whimsical manner; another was most intolerant of differing opinions. But we students felt they were all men. They were all competent. Two were great scholars. They were perfectly devoted to their profession. They were easy of approach. . . .[2]

Or as Barzun points out:

They can differ in endless unpredictable ways. You can take the halt, the lame, the blind, men with speech defects or men who cannot be heard above a whisper, gross and repulsive men (at first) like my blessed mathematics instructor; men who are lazy and slow, who are bright and unstable, or incorrigible enfants terribles; you can even risk some who are deficient in learning, and join them to form an admirable as well as an induplicable faculty. . . .[3]

The point is obvious. Students are personalities, not learners simply of a science; teachers also are personalities, not alone specialized purveyors of a science. Even were the ends of teaching simply purveying data, the personality structure of the student and of the teacher are inescapable elements in the situation. When the goals of instruction are broadened the nontechnical aspects of the professorial art rise to dominating importance.

The Changing Educational Scene. If ever the role of the professor was acceptably defined as that of a "learned man expounding his learning," that role is certainly inadequate in modern American higher education. The educational milieu within which the professor operates is undergoing revolutionary changes; changes that have at once complicated his position and subjected him to new standards of performance. Much decrying of the sad state of professorial esteem in America arises from unwillingness to recognize that new professorial obligations have arisen—and hence new criteria of community status.* If the stereotype of the venerable professor ever existed in fact, it is today extinct or dying. The purveyor of rare intellectual champagnes and caviars shares his stall with the bread and potatoes man. As the President's Commission on Higher Education points out,

The idea that vocation is "servile" is certainly long since out-of-date. By broadening the basis of government to include all the people, democracy has made it necessary to give to all citizens the education formerly reserved for a privileged class. There can no longer be a distinction between inferiors, trained only for practical tasks, and superiors trained for government or the professions.[4]

As a result of the steady increases in the amount of knowledge in the physical and social sciences and in the changing concept of the role of higher education, the curriculum of high schools and colleges continues to expand enormously in terms of new subjects and new courses of study. A new kind of student has also come into existence. "Industrial technology increases the demand for technical and practical studies; the conception of democracy has

---

* This would not assume, however, that status *within* the college system rests upon teaching ability.

led to demands for 'education for all'; and the desire to make money has led to demands for increasingly useful and vocational subjects. Schools or departments of business, journalism, engineering, architecture, pharmacy, dentistry, agriculture, mining, forestry, household arts, applied arts, library science, and education were added to large institutions that had already included colleges of liberal arts, medicine, law and theology." [5] And in this connection, the President's Commission emphasizes that, "Few of us can build a richly textured and gracious life without first making a living; cultural values soon take wing when men cannot get and hold jobs." [6]

Insofar as higher education has shifted toward the secular and pragmatic, insofar must the professor face new criteria of judgment and new conceptions of his role. The superficiality of certain expressions of these new standards may be deplored, but in a pragmatic educational milieu the professor can ill afford to rest upon a wisdom which he himself can alone venerate. Yet such a departure from traditional concepts is, for many, an inherently painful change. To these conservative educators the philosophical basis of learning itself is placed in jeopardy. The bodily senses and physical perceptions, they argue, are no substitute for the intellectual life in the pursuit of truth. To be sure, the pace of modern life is fast and perhaps continues to accelerate, but this is all the more reason, it is argued, for preserving an attitude of "academic retreat" and intellectual contemplation.

To others, however, the dynamic character of contemporary society has established the necessity for new and "progressive" ideas in education. To them education must be in the vanguard of change. The ivy covered ivory tower is simply a place for the academic man to hide his head. Not only must the educator himself be alert to the new technological and cultural forces which are changing the face of the earth, but his students must be prepared to live in and contribute to a world which, if not always brave, is indubitably new.

The new role of the professor, consequently, is to be found

somewhere between these extreme views. Its specific characteristics are largely reflective of the new demands of the classroom and these have dual historical roots. Not only has the ideology of higher education shifted, but the role of the professor arose in the ancient formation of the college concept. Its beginnings are in an era when most people worked but few were educated. The college, and the professor, were the agents of "culture" in a world which set sharp distinctions between the cultural and the practical. The college was or has been at various times the surrogate of an intellectual class, a cultured class, and a leisure class. In the classical tradition in which America shared, the college was the training ground for either gentlemen or scholars or both. And the classroom was oriented toward these ends and toward the select body of students pursuing them.

With the rising tide of democratization in higher education, not only has the ideological climate of the college shifted, so also has its curriculum and, of critical importance, its student body. The controversy between genteel, moneyed aristocratic and/or intellectualistic democratic conceptions of higher education is crucial today. Yet in more ways than one the aristocratic concept of higher education has suffered. Not only has the college become less selective in its students on a financial basis but its active purposes have been expanded beyond the demands either of gentility or pure intellectual pursuit. Insofar as the two are separable the college has diminished as a training ground of gentlemen and scholars and grown tremendously as the training place of workers in everyday life. So far has this gone that the conservative view of the college as a place for the few has become an anachronism. Ideologically the battle to open the higher schools was begun and partially won in the nineteenth century; practically, in terms of enrollments, the full force of democratic education is only presently being felt.

As this shift is felt both the goals and structure of college classes change. The college as the trainer of "leaders" is giving way to the education of all normal citizens for usefulness. In this process leaders of educational thought have insisted that the new "practical" approach meant no sacrifice in the older values of higher education. Dewey, for example, completely rejected the dichotomy of "cultural" and "practical," indicating that such a distinction rested on a falsely narrowed conception of life. In a groping and tentative manner American colleges have gone toward the ideal of Dewey in which humanistic values are integrated with the interests and activities in which the mass of men and women are engaged. As Butts states: "It now seems reasonable to suppose that the same historical forces that made democratic schools necessary in the nineteenth century are making democratic colleges a like necessity in the twentieth." [7]

The implications of this shift upon the nature of college teaching are profound. The professor is no longer a community landmark around whom the legends of veneration arise. He is no longer a member in a highly personalized fraternity of colleagues. He is, rather, likely to belong to a large faculty of specialists.[8] He must face not a circle of students but a room or lecture hall of students, most of whom he knows slightly or not at all outside the confines of the classroom. His discussion is addressed to no homogeneous group of seekers after knowledge; popular education means diversity in background, interests, and many levels of intellectual incentives to get a "college education." And perhaps most important of all, and but partially graspable even by professors whose college days were in the twenties, the students whom he faces know that college has a direct bearing upon livelihood, and that marks have a direct bearing upon staying in college. The secular value of college education is most keen when the college becomes an important means of social mobility. And in this milieu the course mark and credit take on a direct economic value.

From this point of view, the American college, of all contemporary social institutions, has become perhaps the most effective device for facilitating the upward social mobility of young persons of underprivileged backgrounds. The desire for some kind of higher education has become a significant trait in our culture, and today the young person "working his way through college" is as much, if not more, respected as the student who basks in the security of a satisfactory parental allowance. In fact, the student who is on his own may, paradoxically enough, enjoy specific advantages over his financially more fortunate colleagues. And not the least of these is to be found in the student-teacher relationship, however impersonal this may be. To the teacher the working or self-supporting student has "proved" himself on other than an academic level and such a demonstration of ability is difficult to overlook when it comes to final grades or letters of recommendation. Thus the subtle blending of the practical with the academic has taken place within the very nature of the contemporary student body. The educational process for many becomes the essence of social and economic opportunity. It lies near the heart of the American Way. For the dispenser of education it poses questions, obligations, doubts and fears. He is forced to wonder at his job. What is he doing? And how well? As Barzun remarks, "sabbatical leaves are provided so you can have your coronary thrombosis off the campus."

In short, however the ends and goals of higher education ultimately may be resolved and defined, the classroom relationship of the professor to his student is the vital link. It lies close to the center of the educational process. We have, rightly or wrongly, oriented our system to the classroom—the stage of action for the professor and his students.

2

THE PROFESSOR AND HIS STUDENTS

THE professor's relationship to his "clientele" has no parallel in other professions. His services are performed upon a group having relatively little power over his economic position or his academic status. In his professorial functions he enjoys a unique personal and professional protection. No other profession is so largely exempt from the potential sanctions invoked by a hostile clientele. Conversely, no other profession stands to gain as little, unless perhaps the clergy, from a well satisfied public. On the other hand, the professor's clients, like those of most professional practitioners, are per se, as laymen, incapable of completely informed judgment of their properties.

Although lay judgments of the college professor, as of most professional practitioners, are in fact persistently and constantly formed, in the professor's case they can be acted upon only in very slight degree. Only in extreme cases of violent antipathy, shock or fear, does a student body effectively retard a teacher's professorial status and development. Only in the utter extremity of delight does a student body materially enhance a professor's status and stimulate the speed of his professional advancement and renown.

Unique also in the ranks of wage earners is the professor's relative protection against standards imposed from above. Neither deans nor college presidents, nor even departmental chairmen usually feel free to inspect the "work" of persons of professorial rank. The professor's right to build his course, to teach his own way, to mark students by his own standards, all these are traditional privileges of the man of learning. In few reputable institutions would administrative officers violate them without fear of insurrection. This exemption is more than a symbol of professorial esteem; it is part of the sacred trappings of academic freedom. The dean's knowledge of Professor X as a classroom man is back-fence knowledge gleaned from "helpful" students and talkative colleagues. The professor, himself, apart from grave instances, can talk to his students and answer to no one. His occupational freedom, insofar as teaching goes, is all but complete. No one "competent" to judge him enters his sanctum.

This is not to say, however, that this element of freedom is necessarily extended into other spheres. In his political life, for example, the professor perhaps more frequently than his other professional colleagues becomes the target for loyalty oath controversies, red-baiting, and other devices calculated to limit or curb freedom of action or expression. But this situation is all but irrelevant to the present discussion of his role in the classroom. It is another problem entirely.

Professor Schneider, in commenting upon what one is almost tempted to label as an element of secrecy surrounding classroom situations, explains the phenomenon in terms of the demands of an obsolete past.

Although in centuries past the promulgators of this "academic sovereignty" high mindedly fought at great personal risk against the encroachments of an absolutist dynastic State or a dogmatic authoritarian Church, or both, "academic sovereignty" now serves but too often as a protective cloak for shabby indifference and inexcusable waste.[1]

That this system is abused no one who has attended or taught in an American college can deny. How widely is it abused? How intentionally? No one may guess. But intelligent students become inured to obviously deficient instruction in which the onus of non-comprehension falls upon their own shoulders.

The Isolation of the Professor. It cannot be said, however, that students do not utilize their vantage point of the classroom for evaluating their professors. No teacher is exempt from the passage of rumor, tips and invectives. But the external effectiveness of these within the student body is unlikely to affect the professor's status, and still less likely to affect his instructional methods. The very nature of the situation proffers reasonable escape from the bites of student criticism, since the student is by virtue of his student status deemed incompetent of judgment. The tangible protection of the classroom is expanded into psychological protection and professorial rationalization. Whether accurate or inaccurate, these devices serve as a reasonable mechanism in the defense of personal integrity. And indeed the professor has no objective means for determining whether or not a student jibe has reasoned justification or is itself a rationalization for inattention, poor work or personal spite.

The vagueness of the psychological "atmosphere" within which the professor operates leads to many paradoxes. It is, for example, probably true that most professors firmly believe themselves to be good teachers. In fact, such an assumption would almost seem to be necessary to a minimum standard of daily mental health. Any alternative would be intolerable. For not to believe in one's teaching ability and to continue to teach presents a regular three-times-a-week nightmare for each course to which one is chained. While it is true that some may leave the profession because of their inability to convince themselves of their teaching competence, or because their rationalizing mechanisms have finally collapsed, for the great majority the culturally sanctioned stereotype of themselves as good teachers keeps them on the job, more or less happily, year in and year out.

Teaching, after all, is a career to which one is committed. To leave it becomes more than a serious matter. It means a break with one's way of life. A kind of ideological marriage has been consummated with the academic world, and divorce, within the tradition of learning, is not to be lightly regarded. Perhaps it is this sense of dedication which permits a teacher's rationalization about himself to go one step further. Not only does he think of himself as a *good* teacher, he is excellent! Who can convince him that he isn't? Certainly there can exist no conclusive evidence to the contrary. The fallacy here, of course, is that he is in a position to set his own standards of excellence, and then, by some peculiarly human twist of logic, measure himself against them. It is not uncommon for a professor to be overheard saying, "Last semester I *really* reached three students. Whenever I can do that I'm more than satisfied." The fact that he had a hundred students in his courses somehow is irrelevant. And the apparent statistical result that he was only 3 per cent effective is translated into positive terms. Yet his colleagues nod sympathetically and in most cases uncritically accept the logic. The ninety-seven students who weren't reached, were the faculty conversation to be continued, would probably be judged unfit for the course anyway, so what does it matter? As a faculty member said recently in one such conversation, "Even the gods find it difficult to fight against stupidity."

The professor, then, is almost completely deprived of any kind of systematic stimulation or criticism which might lead to his increasing competence as a teacher. He works in the dark and is automatically forced into a kind of self back-slapping to bolster his morale. The cultural standards by which success and failure are recognized for the lawyer or doctor, or any other professional man, do not exist for the teacher. His standards are custom made for his own consumption, and personal limitations and inadequacies, if such are recognized, obviously fall outside his self-imposed goals.

This protective shell, however, composed as it is of rationalizations and stereotypes, is not always perfect. The dissatisfied student can often penetrate it and set up long-term irritations and anxieties. And conversely the appreciative student, with a complimentary remark or two, may set in motion a wave of confidence and sense of well-being that lasts for months. That the latter may be an "apple-polisher" or one of the 3 per cent who are "reached" is not pertinent to the argument. The point is that the teacher has no ready means of knowing where he stands with his students. Yet he has the uncomfortable conviction of the importance of his public relations.

The interaction between teacher and student, while superficially limited to the sphere of the professor's intellectual competence, actually, of course, covers an extensive range of experience types and emotional levels. The classroom relationship is formal yet the greatest satisfactions for many professors are in intimate office and home discussions with alert students. Although seemingly specific to subject matter, professor-student relations properly evoke serious effects upon the student's choice of career, his attitudes toward learning, his personal value system and social viewpoint. All this is sum and substance of the professorial role, and even if these aspects are overtly rejected by either student or professor, they are still inherent in the situation. Over and above all these the professor is in some degree a taskmaster and a judge.

On the other side, the professor receives from the student a major source of career satisfaction. Intelligent student response is his source of zest. If he is a professor (not a human variety of gramophone) the caliber of his work in the classroom is heavily dependent upon student thought-ways, attitudes, and articulation. There are few professors who would allege instruction to be a one way process; student and teacher are consistently in complementary and reciprocal relations. The professor who consistently is unintelligible or irrelevant to large numbers of students simply is not participating in the educational process. A comprehension of the student himself is an essential ingredient to professing, an ingredient which is not necessarily achieved through introspective devices or splendid intellectual grasp. It comes to him from the student, by direct processes of communication of ideas and interpenetration of personalities.

Teaching and Research. The students must count and, although few academicians would deny the principle, there is much in the American higher educational system that thwarts both professor and student in gaining rapport. The zest derived from the recognition of important work well done is no substitute for material specie in the professor's life. It is notorious that the effective teacher must be a prolific, if not inspired, writer to gain material satisfactions in the college world.[2] The fact that emphasis upon teaching does not "pay" in the same degree as committee work, research writing, etc., creates a competitive strain upon the teacher's time and talent. The undervaluing of good teaching makes the classroom a secondary field of endeavor for many finely endowed and highly motivated professors. Evidence, however, that the professor takes his classroom responsibilities with seriousness is the fact that teaching and classroom preparations are the biggest items on his weekly time budget.[3] And in an educational milieu where the classroom requires the wedding of knowledge and action, research activities are to some degree complementary to the more direct attentions to the teaching phase of academic life.[4] It is not unlikely, however, that these extra-instructional obligations compete most directly with the establishment of teacher-student rapport which remains a peripheral consideration to many instructors.

More serious perhaps than the frustrations of instructionally minded professors within the college is the commonly accepted practice of professorial appointments. Even for appointments involving nominally full time teaching, the qualifications and training of candidates are scrutinized in terms of special subject matter competence rather than in terms of demonstrated pedagogical skills. This very process of selection affects the preservation of the emasculating assumption that the role of the professor is indeed simply that of the scholarly man of learning. N. Foerster has stated this matter trenchantly:

What we are suffering from today is not so much a trivialized curriculum as a trivialized faculty. The only fundamental way to improve the curriculum is to improve the faculty which designs the curriculum. . . . The quality of the faculty depends, in the unwritten constitution of the state university, upon the administrators who appoint the professors. When a vacancy arises, what sort of professor do they look for? They look, sometimes hastily, more often persistently, for a specialist of high repute; i.e., high repute among other specialists. Incidentally they inquire whether the specialist scholar is also a good teacher or at least not a bad one. Incidentally they consider his personality, being satisfied if it is superficially agreeable. They display no concern for his character so long as he has done nothing scandalous, and they have no interest whatever in the values he lives by. A good professor is simply a good specialist in his particular field. . . . The results are deplorable. Administrators are not pleased with their own handiwork, students can admire only a few of their teachers, and even the faculty of specialists is aware that specialism is not enough.[5]

And as Foerster so directly states, weakness in the college as an educational instrument arises not through technical incompetence but in the weakness of the professor in his role as a communicant and his weakness in those ill-defined but invaluable by-products which transform the outpouring of knowledge into effective teaching.

Similarly the doctor's degree has come to serve as an easy standard and ready criterion of teaching competence. Of the Ph.D. phenomenon much has been written and much deplored. Its meaning is at best indistinct. Yet as Barzun bitterly points out, it "has become the union card of the American college teacher." [6] Its persistence in the educational system rests upon two theories, neither of which bear any relationship to teaching. On the one hand is the feeling of colleges and universities that they are obligated to contribute to the store of existing knowledge (and hence must employ scholars who have proved themselves by going through the Ph.D. mill), and on the other hand is the assumption that all teachers must sooner or later, for better or worse, become research people. Such thinking obviously ignores the student. In fact, it frequently operates to his positive disadvantage in that the instructor who tries to teach and earn his degree at the same time is presented with a conflict of values all too readily resolved in favor of the dissertation. But this is only a small part of the question. The confusion in values is brought sharply into focus when the degree winning treatise which will perhaps be read by only a handful of scholars is more highly valued than the efforts of a first rate teacher who year after year reaches several hundred enthusiastic and appreciative students. For the latter contribution there is no "proof," no tangible evidence of success. In fact, such a teacher may, by all existing criteria of rank, degrees, publications, etc., be judged a failure.

The relationship of teaching to research in the scheme of professorial activities has vast and far-reaching implications. Under the system of American higher education any teacher knows instinctively that his chances of getting ahead academically are enormously enhanced if he is at the same time a productive scholar. This means research. And the battle for hours is on. The competition, however, is not merely for time. One's interest is at stake, and there is a real difference between research which is carried out in the interest of teaching and a relative neglect of teaching in the interest of research. Here again the process of rationalization plays an important role. While the best teachers are inevitably engaged in the search for new knowledge, it requires only a slight deviation from logic for a professor to convince himself that any kind of research automatically makes him a better teacher. Once this premise has been firmly established, the central interest of the professor finds its place in research activities and not in teaching.

Yet our colleges and universities expect both types of effort from their faculties—and generally simultaneously from each member. There have been, to be sure, criticisms leveled against this system, but as long as teaching ability can be only imperfectly recognized (even by the teacher himself) while research results in satisfyingly tangible printed papers, the latter will be more highly valued by both teachers and academic administrators. Thus one of the very few objective criteria of professional competence potentially militates against students and the central purpose of higher education. If a "teacher" has neither the skill nor the interest in translating to students the essential meanings of masses of data from the laboratories or from the inert shelves of the libraries, he is no longer a teacher, and the institution which shelters him no longer is in the business of education.

This is not to say, of course, that the research man is consequently a poorer teacher than his non-researching colleague. On the contrary, the evidence seems to point in the other direction, for members of the Brooklyn College faculty who had successfully engaged in research activities were judged better teachers than those who had no published works to their credit. (See Chapter 9.)

The American college teacher, in short, is a man of many roles. He sits uncomfortably in his professorial chair and views the passing scene with some alarm. His traditional protective coloring no longer is as effective. His academic retreat is more and more exposed. Yet his students come in increasing numbers. What he does about them and for them takes on a new significance, and what they think begins to count.

3

THE THEORY AND PRACTICE
OF STUDENT EVALUATIONS

SINCE the professor's ivory tower is crumbling, some medium
for the expression of student reactions to college teaching is
indeed indicated. Even within his uniquely protected role as a
purveyor of higher education, the professor, in the last analysis,
is forced into the realistic position of taking into at least some
account the impact of his activities upon students. Whether the
students be stupid, biased, disinterested or simply bored—or even
if they appear enthralled—the professorial concern remains. Teaching is not a one-sided coin, however tradition may have attempted
to make it so. Both expositor and learner are involved. There is
both action and reaction. Since all this is fact, there is a growing
awareness that it should at last be looked at squarely. This awareness has already led to a number of measurements of student reactions, and their import is discussed in this chapter.

Intuition and the development of subtle insights may to be
sure provide certain skilled teachers with a clear view of student
reactions. For such teachers there is probably no problem. And
even the conscientious teacher may, if adequately motivated, adopt

an unsubtle, frontal attack as has one professor covered by the present inquiry.

I have always recognized student opinion as a valuable guide to the teacher. For more than twenty years I have asked my students to give me anonymous written comments at the end of each course. My teaching methods and course organization have definitely been influenced and guided by such comments.

By and large, however, the average professor appears to perform his rituals of course preparations, to meet his classes with fair regularity, and to hope for the best.

From the student point of view no such individually motivated, though constructive, possibilities exist for examining the neglected side of the teaching coin. The professor's students, like consumers within the contemporary economy, are relatively unorganized. Students may flock to the teacher whose courses enjoy a reputation for sense and value, much as housewives will patronize the butcher who fairly trades in quality products. But boycotts at either level are rarely effective when dissatisfactions arise. The staples of education are no less varied than those for the table, and the users of both products enjoy limited choices by virtue of the daily necessities of use.

The analogy begins to fall apart when recent trends in American higher education are considered. Particularly under conditions of the expanding democratization of student bodies, is it difficult for students, even were they equipped to judge, to select their own professors. Not only are the bread and butter courses typically taught by many teachers, but the exigencies of schedules make choices all but impossible. At the graduate level, or in the European university, the impact of student opinion as manifest through course selection may be important and significant, but the typical undergraduate situation today presents a very different picture. Certain broad subject matters must be covered before the diploma is granted, and the courses which will yield the necessary number and distribution of academic credits become the central consideration. What teachers happen to be acquired during this process tends to be a matter of chance, and frequently, from the student point of view, a question of luck.

Even the "luckiest" students have little opportunity for articulating their good fortune, and only in the rarest instances do the unlucky ones resort to rebellion. The matter typically reduces itself to student gossip, "Try to get into so-and-so's course," or "Don't get hooked into his section—he's terrible." But such gossip as an effective means of social control is largely impotent. Certainly as a device through which the level of college teaching might reasonably be raised, it has neither specific meaning nor long-run utility.

Some systematic means of tapping student reaction is indicated. If the student is to speak up, he must be given an instrument.

Student Ratings and Their Objectives. There are several instances in which the students have been allowed to be heard. Informal student ratings of teachers are probably as old as the teacher-student relationship itself. Even the formal student evaluation of a faculty is not a new phenomenon in higher education. "The upsurge of interest in college instruction is one of the most remarkable educational phenomena of the postwar period," according to Dean Cooper of the University of Minnesota.[1] Growing out of the peculiarly "protected" position of the college professor, the need for such information as the rating scale can furnish has been felt both by college administrators and by instructors themselves. Thus, student evaluation scales and testing procedures have developed in response to two different yet both highly practical objectives: first, as an administrative guide to such questions as promotion and dismissal of faculty members, and second, as an instrument for improving the quality of instruction.

As early as 1922, the School of Education of Oklahoma A & M, in an effort to obtain some supervision of college teaching, distributed questionnaires among the student body, guaranteeing that the "material will be used in a confidential way, no one seeing it except the instructor concerned and the dean."[2] Among the most recent attempts to use student evaluations as administrative aids is an experiment at the University of Michigan,[3] said to be the first such step ever taken by an American university as a part of top-level policy. First used in 1948, the instrument was considered so helpful as to be continued "for at least five years, and, probably, permanently." Student opinion with regard to the five lowest rated faculty members was found to correspond closely with the opinion of department heads, and steps were reported already under way to release or reassign these men.

In general, however, surveys which have been undertaken for administrative purposes have met with strong faculty resistances on the grounds that student ratings are in danger of being misinterpreted, that students are not qualified to judge the competence of their instructors, that the ratings are but one criterion, among many others, of teaching effectiveness. More popular with faculty members has been the student survey of teaching ability which seeks only to inform the college professor of his effect upon his audience, in order that he may re-evaluate and improve his techniques in the light of student criticism. The report of the Committee on College and University Teaching of the American Association of University Professors states this position clearly: [4]

It is the committee's belief that the almost universal failure of these rating experiments has been due to the use of untactful and injudicious procedure. Student criticism and ratings ascertained by presidents, deans, or even heads of departments without the advice or consent of the teachers concerned, have not proved fruitful of good results and are not likely to do so. But such criticisms or ratings obtained for the information of the instructor, in accordance with a procedure which he approves, are likely to be advantageous to him.

Indeed the experience at Brooklyn College re-enforced the opinion of the AAUP Committee, for from the inception of the study, the faculty as a whole submitted willingly to examination by the student body. When even greater demands were made upon them, Brooklyn College professors gave striking evidence of their active support of and deep interest in the project. For three out of every four professors responded to a mailed question-naire regarding their reactions to the student evaluations (see Chapter 10). That most of the responses were highly favorable and that among the favorable responses were both high- and low-rated professors is compelling evidence of the good will of the Brooklyn College faculty. Thus, Wilson [5] reports that the "sole purpose" of the student ratings at the University of Wash-ington "was to give the individual instructor information that might be of value to him in increasing the effectiveness of his work. It seems unwise to endanger this purpose by any action that would seem to impute to the appraisals a validity that they cannot be shown to possess. At the present time, the information collected has its greatest value when it is studied by the instructor concerned for the sake of extracting from it all possible help."

The best-known experiment in the field of student evaluations of college professors is the series conducted at Purdue University under the direction of H. H. Remmers. It is perhaps noteworthy that the focus of the Purdue studies has always been the improve-ment of teaching through the teacher's knowledge of his effect upon his students. As Professor Remmers [6] has put it:

The Purdue Rating Scale for Instructors was not designed and is not meant to evaluate teaching efficiency from the standpoint of the ad-ministrator. It is designed to measure the student's prejudices as an important aspect of the teacher-student relationship; important, that is, in determining the learning process. From this point of view it would be a wholly illegitimate use of the scale to use it as a basis for promotion or demotion of teachers. Future investigation may show it to be more or less valid even for such purposes, but at present its only legitimate function is to enable the teacher better to adjust his pro-cedure to that "human nature" which Protzman believes to be the only constant in an educational world of change. The teacher is to see him-self as the students see him.

Measurable Teaching Attributes. The first and perhaps the most serious problem in planning an evaluation of a faculty is the selec-tion of teaching characteristics or traits to be evaluated. Surprisingly enough, among the great number of possible qualities that make an excellent teacher, there seems to be considerable agreement on a limited number of the most important ones. This is true even when students, as reported by Clinton [7] and Boussfield [8] are given complete freedom and instructed merely to list, in order of importance, the qualities which in their opinion are the "most desirable in a college professor." [9] Thus, in twelve studies [10] conducted in various institutions during the past twenty-five years, thirty-eight different qualities of good teaching were selected. When, however, comparisons are made among the twelve sets of criteria, there appears to be near consensus on a relatively small number of components of good teaching. Ten of the twelve studies selected knowledge of the subject and sympathetic attitude and interest in students as important teaching qualities. On the other hand, a number of such miscellaneous characteristics as cheerfulness, understanding of human nature, good social mixer, patience, etc., appeared in only one or two isolated instances. Closest agreement appeared to focus around fourteen attributes of good teaching. These were selected or used for study in at least four of the twelve projects and are listed in Table 1 in order of the number of times selected.

It should be pointed out that the twelve studies cited above are approximately evenly divided between investigations into what constitutes good teaching or what are the important qualities of an excellent teacher, and investigations which push beyond the identification of these qualities into student evaluations of the teaching competence of their instructors on the basis of selected criteria of good teaching. Methodologically the two types of investigation present some interesting contrasts. Thus, in seeking to define teaching ability investigators have relied on various sample types and sizes. Odom based his selection of twelve traits on the opinions of a combination of 26 teachers and 121 students; Smith used as subjects 100 students in educational sociology; Davis, 76 students in two education courses; Clinton, 177 general students; Breed, a committee of four members of the faculty and five students; Boussfield, 61 undergraduates; Reed, a small sample of college administrators. In contrast, studies involving individual teacher ratings, whether for administrative or self-improvement purposes, cannot afford to rely on anything less than an adequate sampling of student opinion.

TABLE 1

QUALITIES OF GOOD TEACHING AS USED IN A SAMPLE OF STUDIES

Quality	Number of Studies
Knowledge of Subject	10
Sympathetic attitude toward and interest in students	10
Interest in subject, enthusiasm	7
Appearance	7
Tolerance, broad-mindedness, liberality	7
Interesting presentation, personality to put course across	6
Sense of humor, sense of proportion	6
Stimulating intellectual curiosity	5
Organization	5
Personality	5
Fairness	5
Sincerity, honesty, moral character	4
Speaking ability	4
Clear explanations	4

Again, for obvious reasons, greater rigidity in the structuring of the questionnaire is necessary where student evaluations of teacher performance are sought than in the construction of a list of ideal teaching traits. In the latter case, for example, students are frequently asked merely "to contribute a frank and explicit statement concerning 'My Ideal Teacher.'" [11] Where evaluations are sought, however, it is usually necessary, for reasons of comparability, that each student rate his teacher on the same set of criteria. Not only the criteria to be rated, but standards for rating the separate traits, are usually provided. Thus, in this kind of project, the questionnaire or instrument is typically a series of scales. The scale used in the present study is discussed and reproduced in Chapter 5.

Objections Common to Student Evaluations of Faculties

Reliability. Many dissatisfactions with the practice of student ratings have been voiced, and the grounds for dissatisfaction have usually centered around the problems of reliability; i.e., the ability of students to make unbiased judgments of a teacher's performance. This is the crucial objection, whether the specific criticism is directed at younger students, less successful students, students of a particular sex, or at all students in general. Yet, for each type of objection there is considerable documentation to discount any belief in the distortion of student judgment by such factors. Grades, for example, have been shown to bear little, if any, relationship to a student's ratings. Starrack compared the marks given a student with his ratings of the instructor responsible for those marks and obtained a coefficient of correlation "small enough to be disregarded." (.15 ± .031.) Similarly, Remmers [12] found the relation between students' marks and their attitudes toward instructors to be negligible (.070).

The effect of "maturity" of students on their responses has also been measured [13] by comparing the ratings of freshmen, sophomores, juniors and seniors. Remmers concludes, as a result of these comparisons, that "the differences are relatively quite unimportant as compared with the resemblances among the four classes."

Considering the familiar and long-standing aversion to large classes, student ratings are also surprisingly consistent between instructors of small and large groups. Again, at Purdue,[14] ratings of instructors were obtained at the end of the school term over a period of three semesters from carefully matched classes in trigonometry. Each teacher had the same number of large and small classes; yet, there was scarcely any difference between the ratings given an instructor by small groups and by large groups.[15] Similarly, Starrack [16] reports that although "the ratings given by small classes (less than seven) and by large classes (more than fifty) tended consistently to be lower than those given by classes ranging in the size between these extremes, the differences were small enough to be disregarded."

The problem of halo effect must also be considered in studies involving the use of rating scales. Halo effect is the tendency to be influenced in making a specific judgment by a general impression of the individual being judged. Unfortunately, while the existence of this tendency is generally recognized, its measurement is extremely complex and involves the correlation, for each instructor, of each trait with each of the other traits. Stalnaker and Remmers [17] calculated such a series of intercorrelations for one instructor and obtained an average intercorrelation of .453± .057 when corrected for errors due to unreliability of the ratings. "Clearly this indicates a gratifying absence of halo effect. One would expect *some* positive correlation among these traits if there were *no* halo effect whatsoever. The amount is at present indeterminate." [18] Using the same procedure, Starrack [19] obtained a mean correlation coefficient of .47. "By another method based upon the differences between the scores on the highest scoring trait and on the lowest scoring trait, it was clearly shown that, while halo effect may be operative in the case of the scale used in this investigation, it does not prohibit the student from exercising considerable discrimination between the different traits on the scale. The reliability of students' judgments in rating the personal fitness and teaching ability of their instructors expressed by the scale seems to be as high as the reliability of standardized achievement scales and the most commonly used intelligence tests." Again, Remmers,[20] using the Spearman-Brown prophecy formula, estimated that with 100 to 120 student evaluations of an instructor, the Purdue Rating Scale is as reliable as "the best standardized mental and educational tests available."

Validity. Two types of student rating procedures were distinguished earlier. The first has as its objective the identification of good and poor instructors as a basis for administrative action. The second type of survey, of which the present inquiry is an example, seeks merely to acquaint each instructor with the degree of his acceptance by his audience. In this latter context, the question of validity is irrelevant, for validity is concerned with student ratings as an accurate measure of teaching ability; that is, a rating scale would be considered a valid instrument only if it elicited from the students the same judgment of a given instructor as would be obtained from an expert judge in the field of education. It should be evident that the goal of such studies as the present investigation was the gathering of student opinions for their own intrinsic value and without regard to any objective standard of teaching excellence. Nevertheless, some evidence exists in support of the hypothesis that student ratings do have some validity as tests of teaching ability. Starrack[21] reports that "in over 75 per cent of the cases studied in this phase of the investigation, the opinions of the students and of three experts in methods were found to be in close agreement, although in the remaining 25 per cent of the cases studied the divergence of opinion was great enough to indicate that either the judgment of the experts or that of the students could not be trusted." At the University of Washington, Guthrie[22] found "more consistency in student judgments of the faculty than in faculty judgments of the faculty. It is quite possible," he suggests, "that a just and objective method of measuring the worth of a man as a teacher should take student judgment into account." Finally, Breed[23] at the University of Chicago reported a high correlation between fifty-six faculty members and a hundred students on the qualities of good teaching.

Whether or not the rating scale can legitimately be used as "a just and objective measure of the worth of a man as a teacher," its value as a mirror of student reactions is unquestioned. Says William R. Wilson,[24] "Only by accident will the teaching of a man ignorant of the reactions of his class be effective." As documentation he presents the results of a repetition of the University of Washington survey six months following the initial rating of instructors:

On those topics on which the instructors had made a thoughtful and systematic effort to improve, the June averages were about twenty-five centile points higher than in December. . . . A considerable number of the instructors received information that, they felt, justified a drastic reorganization of their courses. Few received information that they were not able to use to the betterment of their work.

Similarly, Patterson [25] reported an improvement in teaching performance among the faculty of the School of Education at Oklahoma A & M College during the year following the conduct of a faculty evaluation survey. And Starrack [26] found that teachers' ratings increased "quite materially" with each successive rating over a two-year period. This evidence of improvement of faculty performance—in the students' eyes, at least—is, in a very real sense, the best validation possible for this type of survey which has as its goal the improvement of teaching through an awareness of student opinions. Louella Cole [27] has given forceful expression to the point of view that student ratings are both reliable and valuable:

The students are the consumers of teaching, and they know what they can and cannot consume, even if they are foggy about the reasons. Students admittedly cannot analyze teaching ability into its elements nor do they often have a clear standard of what constitutes good teaching, but they do not need to have either. They can answer specific questions about their own reactions, and that is all any scale asks them to do. The interpretation of the results is not their business. . . . The idea that college students, especially upperclassmen, cannot give reliable opinions about a teacher with whom they have spent from thirty to sixty hours is rather ridiculous. It is much easier to fool one's colleague than one's students. . . . There are many uses for student ratings, provided these are handled with common sense. Students are not fools. They see, hear, discuss, and think about every little thing that goes on in the classroom. The information they can give is worth having. It does not tell all there is to know about a teacher, but it is good evidence concerning those points upon which only students are in a position to testify.

A Theoretical Justification. Without attempting, however, to resolve the problem of student capability in judging the total effectiveness of his instruction, it is clear that inescapable obligations rest upon the professor in return for his relative immunity from criticism.

It is not our intention to make any claim in support of the ability of any student body to make an objective and valid analysis of a faculty. That, it must be re-emphasized, is not the point at issue. The real point, rather, lies in the assumption that student judgments and evaluations, however immature, biased or prejudiced they may be, contribute to the complex of realities in any teaching situation. The professor is dealing with human beings and even in the classroom, where he exercises a high degree of control and authority, he cannot separate these "beings" from their prejudices and gratifications. The students' ideas of good teaching, of ideal instructional characteristics, are inevitably part and parcel of any teacher's daily routine. He may attempt to ignore their reality, he may consciously or subconsciously isolate himself, but it is nevertheless clear that his increased effectiveness as a teacher can only be gained through a critical recognition of this element in the educational process—an element which has too often been studiously overlooked and ignored.

This tendency toward professional escapism dies hard. It is deeply rooted and productive of many sophistries. It is, for example, often argued that the student is indeed incapable of valuing the scholarship of a professor by virtue of his "enforced" participation in the painful process of thinking. He not only may be influenced by personal bias or prejudice, but he may project his own insufficiencies upon the professor. In any individual instance these processes may be at work. That they are sufficient in most instances in so thoroughly infecting a student body as to remove all objectivity is extremely doubtful. And, indeed, most studies of student evaluations of faculty have found a high degree of conscientiousness reflected. But even were the student demonstrably incapable of seasoned and objective judgment, it is vital that the student speak. Learning does not take place upon automatons; it takes place within students with their biases, misconceptions and resistances. Effective teaching can rely on no standardized system of techniques and scholarship; it must take into account the peculiar nature of the student. *What the student hears is more important than what the professor says; what the student sees is more important than what the professor does.* The student's definition of the professor is as tangible a part of the instructional situation as are the skills and knowledge of the professor. Whatever the goal of instruction, a sound working relationship between student and professor is necessary for the fulfillment of that goal. As Barzun suggests,

Teaching . . . is a developing emotional situation. It takes two to teach and from all we know of great teachers the spur from the class to the teacher is as needful an element as the knowledge it elicits.[28]

And Sir John Adams re-emphasizes the point when he says that "education is brought about by the interaction of character upon character." [29]

The importance of professorial awareness of student attitudes toward instruction is made the greater by contemporary trends in higher education. The same conditions that have made the teaching role in the American college complex have also made the systematic analysis of student thinking toward instruction more vital. Higher education has come out into the open; the new pragmatic demands, the functional and utilitarian concept of higher education, coupled with a heightened impersonality in the classroom and heterogeneity in class composition, intensify the need for and difficulty of catalyzing student thinking.

Yet a consensus on this point among contemporary educators is far from being reached. Among the professors who came within the scope of the study reported in this volume was one who stormed back with the comment, "The whole idea is a miserable concession to an age that is more and more moving away from respect for authority." Here is a man, then, whose roots are deeply imbedded in another age. He is the spokesman for the maintenance and restoration of academic "rights." And he still has many followers.

If, however, the popular democratic and pragmatic concept of a college education is worth pursuit, then student definition of the classroom situation is worth knowing. Without this knowledge the professor may well be a voice crying in the wilderness. Without *expression* by the student there can be no *impression* for the professor. Either we change our concept of higher education or the professor must include in his definition of the classroom situation his own reflection as seen in the students' eyes.

4

Practical Application: A Case Example

DURING the past twenty-five years the teacher rating scale, as we have seen, has come into considerable prominence. Its literature ranges from detailed statistical reports to bitter controversies over its utility and desirability. But the very generality of the increasing interest attests to the need for such studies. Too often, however, the various local experiments, while they may attract a flurry of newspaper notices, exert only local influence, and the practical and pedestrian aspects of the project, which might be of enormous help to other studies, fail to be recorded and are quickly forgotten. Here, consequently, is a specific example of the way in which the need for student evaluations was recognized in one institution, together with a "history" of the project. It is quite possible that such an account in its various aspects is, by virtue of the personal (and possibly explosive) nature of its subject matter, fully as important to further research along these lines as is its methodology.

Unlike the physical or natural sciences, any empirical project in social research has only begun to solve its problems with the development of a method or instrument. By definition, no inquiry involving human relationships can be conducted in vacuo, and a similar logic carries us one step further in emphasizing the total social or cultural situation within which human relationships occur. Certainly in the case of the problem presently under discussion, it would have been impossible even to conceive the research details without reference to the larger institutional setting. Many groups and interested persons are almost automatically involved, and it has, consequently, seemed desirable to reconstruct in some detail these broader aspects of the project prior to a discussion of its methodology.

The Student Body Takes the Initiative. Initiated by the student body of Brooklyn College, the student reaction survey grew into a cooperative enterprise of some scope. Brooklyn students, faculty, and administration, and personnel from the Rutgers research office all became parties in the venture. The project itself developed indirectly from a survey conducted by Brooklyn students working within the public opinion unit of the college's Bureau of Government Research. This study was to throw light on the influence of course content as against the instructor's teaching ability in student selection of courses.

The real story of that enterprise, however, began in the spring term of 1945, with the creation of a special student Committee on the Improvement of Teaching. According to an article in the student publication, the *Brooklyn College Vanguard,* the student committee had succeeded in obtaining seventeen hundred student signatures to a "petition requesting an official system of student-teacher rating"; it had compiled and sent to the teachers concerned the results of an experiment which sought to obtain from students in approximately fifty classes "concrete and constructive suggestions for the improvement of the respective courses"; and it had sent to all members of the faculty a sample copy of a student-formulated rating blank "for the purpose of obtaining constructive criticism for its improvement."

Revised and administered in two departments, the statement of objectives of the student-conducted survey is here presented as evidence that, whatever changes have been made in the form and scope of the survey, its broad aims have remained largely the same from its inception by the student committee to its culmination in this report.

Purpose of the Survey

(From the report of the Student Committee on the Improvement of Teaching to faculty members who partook in the teaching evaluating experiment.)

The survey was conducted with the aim of providing some instrument for communicating the views of his students, concerning his teaching, to the instructor. Motivation for this aim may be found in the every day experience of the students on the committee. They have observed that many teachers are unaware to what degree their teaching duties are carried out, since there is no practical device to obtain and examine student opinion of their teaching. The project of the Student Council Committee on The Improvement of Teaching is merely an attempt to present to the instructor information as to how their students view them as individuals and their opinion of the success he achieves in teaching. The Committee is of the opinion that it is essential for an instructor to have a knowledge of this student reaction if he is to reexamine intelligently his methods of instruction. It is felt that the psychological relationship existing between the teacher and the student is of the utmost import in the achievement of greater success in teaching. Besides obtaining specific constructive suggestions for improving instruction, one may also gain from this report a good picture of the type of student-teacher relationship existent. In presenting you with this information it is the hope of this Committee that you as an individual instructor, may better learn what the students hope and look for in taking your course. It is desired that the information that we present will aid you in a better understanding of the students' values and interests so that you may present your material to them in such terms that are familiar and significant to them. It is the aim of the committee to help you identify yourself with the interest of your students and so enable you to convey to them your own system of values more successfully.

The Committee would like to make clear its belief that techniques of teaching can never become substitutes to the slightest degree for scholarly competence; but it is also believed that academic scholarship must be useful functionally. That is, in order for knowledge to be of value to the student, it first must be conveyed to him so that he understands it. To aid in achieving this, a picture of the student's reaction to your teaching is presented to you, not in a spirit of destructive or innocuous griping, but rather for the purpose of supplying *constructive* and concrete suggestions for possible means of improving your present methods of instruction. It is not hoped or expected that all instructors will rate equally high on all questions. The Committee does not expect a situation where the calibre of teaching is perfect and the instructors infallible individuals. It is realized that teaching is a very difficult and complex task. Also understood is the fact that it is a highly personal and individual process. Consequently, these compiled suggestions and criticisms should be viewed by each particular instructor in the light of his own personal experience. It is anticipated that when the teacher is confronted with day-to-day problems in teaching, he will, as a result of this information, have a better insight into the causes for his successes and failures. This information should not be considered as conclusive, and the committee, realizing there may be possible deficiencies present in this survey, suggest that you personally investigate further in order to verify the data.

The Faculty Approves. Student demands did not go unheeded. Soon after the receipt of the petition, a faculty committee was appointed to investigate the field of student evaluations of teaching and its feasibility on the Brooklyn College campus.

Having decided, on the basis of past experience in other institutions and on the basis of meetings with student and faculty representatives, that the survey should be conducted by an off-the-campus research agency, the faculty committee made contact with the Sociology Department of Rutgers University. At the request of the chairman of the Brooklyn College Faculty Committee the Rutgers group drew up a "Proposal to Study Student Opinion of Teachers in Brooklyn College." The proposal, prepared early in 1946, was submitted by the committee to the members of the Faculty Council, together with a report of the committee's findings and recommendations.

Proposal to Study Student Opinion
of Teachers in Brooklyn College

The purpose of this research is to improve the quality of college teaching by exploring a hitherto neglected aspect of the subject—student thought and attitudes.

Higher education today is entering a new era. Unanticipated responsibilities are ahead. Old traditions are being re-examined. The quality of its teaching is one of the basic considerations.

Final judgment or evaluation of the qualities which constitute effective college teaching should be based on many lines of evidence. In proposing to explore the field of student judgment there is no thought of suggesting that it is more important than many other bases of evaluation, such as years of training, teaching experience, published writing, and so on. However, a number of important considerations suggest this as a fruitful area of research.

1. Any appraisal of effective teaching which neglects the reactions of the students themselves would appear to be unbalanced.
2. It would be in line with the tendency in educational theory to view the educational process as a reciprocal relationship between teacher and student.
3. Research in this area has been comparatively neglected. Popularity polls have been conducted by student newspapers, but these are at best crude and unscientific. They pay little attention to sampling procedures and validating criteria.
4. Personnel research by large industries in which employees rate their supervisors points to the practical applicability of data of this type.
5. Research techniques in the fields of public opinion and sociometry now exist which could be adapted to yield valid results in a research of this nature.

In short, the need exists for research in this field, and appropriate methods for doing it are available.

The objectives of this research are two-fold:

1. To obtain student ratings on all teachers in terms of: student-teacher relations, knowledge of the field, class-room personality, teaching ability, etc.
2. To obtain from the student full statements as to the qualities, traits and capacities which they think characterize the ideal teacher.

Since such data could very seriously affect the positions of the teachers if put to improper use, they should be strictly controlled on the basis of a predetermined policy clearly understood by the Faculty and Administration of Brooklyn College.

The various steps proposed in carrying out this project are as follows:

1. Open interviewing among a small sample of students on another campus. This will serve to determine the details of the questionnaire form.
2. Pre-testing the questionnaire, also on a different campus, until validity has been established.
3. Collection of the data:
   a) Our aim would be to get a questionnaire filled out by every student at Brooklyn College. To do this we would need the fullest cooperation of the Administration of the College.
   b) Methods would be devised to provide places on the campus where the students could fill out the questionnaires with complete anonymity. The use of the checklist, as in elections, would serve as a control against successive voting by the same student.
   c) Successive balloting periods, preceded by reminder notices to those still remaining unchecked, would be continued until the complete poll is taken.
   d) While the questionnaire would be anonymous each respondent would be asked to indicate his class, age, sex, veteran status, work experience, major field of study, etc. to permit detailed analysis of the responses of different types of students.
4. The data thus acquired will be coded and transferred to IBM cards and tabulation sheets to facilitate statistical analysis.

The report will present two different types of findings. On the one hand, detailed data and "scores" will be given for each faculty member. On the other hand, the patterns of attributes which students look for in the effective teacher will be shown in some detail according to the subject matter taught.

The implications of these findings to American colleges as a whole will be pointed out. Such implications will, of course, bear in mind the particular characteristics of Brooklyn College, metropolitan, non-resident, etc. Obviously, similar research of this character in other colleges would yield more generally applicable results.

The following questions are illustrative of the types which the analysis might answer:

1. Do students in different fields vary in their estimates of the effective teacher?
2. Does freshman evaluation of teaching differ from senior evaluation?
3. Do superior, average and poor students differ in their estimates of effective teaching?
4. To what extent does the degree of student participation in the class-room color teacher evaluations?
5. Does work experience influence student's estimates of teaching?
6. What are the differences in opinions of teachers of elective and required courses?
7. Are the evaluations of students who expect to continue in any way different?

The reactions of the Faculty Committee to the research proposal and the care with which the entire project was debated and considered (a point of probably universal significance in studies of this kind) are well illustrated by excerpts from their report.

Excerpts from Report of the Faculty Committee on Student Evaluations

To the members of Faculty Council:

In response to a communication to Faculty from the Student Council Committee on the Improvement of Teaching, enclosing a petition signed by 1700 students, Faculty Council authorized on *May 10, 1945* the appointment by the President of a Faculty Committee to study the question of student evaluation of teaching.

Your committee recommends that:

1. Authorization be given by the Faculty Council for the conduct of a survey of student evaluation of teachers by the Social Research Office of Rutgers University or by some other qualified, off-the-campus group.
2. A faculty-student committee of four faculty members elected by Faculty Council—one from each of the following groups: arts, humanities, sciences, social sciences, and four student members selected by Student Council be set up to serve as liaison between the faculty, students and the research agency. This committee will also keep the faculty and student body informed of the progress of the study.
3. Because of the highly experimental nature of the project, the results

of this survey as they pertain to the individual instructor shall be made known only to that instructor. Your committee believes that the individual teacher can benefit from the criticism that a scientifically conducted survey affords.

4. Since another aspect of the survey, as indicated in the attached proposal from Rutgers, is the determination of the "patterns of attributes which students look for in the effective teacher—according to the subject matter taught," the summary data should be made available to the college community. Your committee believes that these findings will prove as valuable for the improvement of teaching as the rating of individual instructors.

5. The college administration be requested to seek available funds to conduct the survey. Your committee feels that a Foundation devoted to promoting projects of an educational nature may be ready to grant the necessary funds.

The Administrative Officers Carry Out the Recommendations of Students and Faculty. Early in 1947, in response to a request by the President of the College, the Carnegie Foundation for the Advancement of Teaching approved a grant for the purpose of investigating student evaluations of the quality of teaching at Brooklyn College. Shortly thereafter, Rutgers University definitely committed itself to undertake this project. The terms of the agreement between Rutgers and Brooklyn College were outlined in a letter addressed to the Dean of Studies of the latter institution, excerpts from which are reproduced here.

Letter Outlining Plan of Survey

Our approach to the problem would tentatively involve the following steps:

1. Completion of a questionnaire by each regularly enrolled day student (about 8,000) evaluating five of his instructors. This would entail about 40,000 evaluations. (Of this number some 8,000 [one-fifth] would not be used in drawing individual instructor ratings since about 100 instructors are to be omitted, though all must be included in the sampling.)

2. Resulting data would be placed on IBM cards and appropriate sortings made to reveal the distribution of student attitude toward

each instructor in a number of relevant characteristics (not over 12).

3. The average scores for each instructor upon each characteristic would be presented to the instructor concerned in such a way that he could see his position relative to the entire faculty.

4. A sample of the evaluations would be used for purposes of intensive analysis relating evaluations to characteristics both of the student evaluating and to the faculty member evaluated.

Clearly from the size of the job before us, it will not be possible to make either extensive or intensive analysis of the student responses to individual faculty members. While spontaneous responses from students are exceedingly valuable, the sheer volume of work makes it necessary to limit our questions to controlled items that will be precoded. While qualitative comments may be collected, we cannot expect to give them systematic analysis.

It is our thought that not more than twelve key questions calling for evaluation on different aspects of the classroom-teaching situation will suffice. (Financially such limitation is unavoidable.) This will involve the student's grading of the instructor in the following areas, at a minimum:

1) Apparent adequacy of instructor's knowledge of his subject.
2) Adequacy of classroom techniques, lecturing, guiding discussion, etc.
3) Instructor's attitude toward the student, his conscientiousness, fairness, etc.
4) Instructor's attitude toward his job, interest in work, etc.

In addition to the above, we anticipate collecting from each student from five to ten attitude statements on problems not immediately touching the individual faculty member, but closely allied with instructional problems. Examples of such problems would be attitudes regarding adequacy of student advisory and counselling services, attitudes toward freedom in selection of courses, and others which may be suggested. Apart from the attitudinal questions, we expect to acquire information from the student on certain of his own characteristics relevant to the character of attitudes. Such characteristics would include student's age, sex, year in college, veteran status, marital status, grade average, curriculum, and others to be decided.

We would expect also to procure, presumably from administrative files, certain background characteristics of instructors which should be related to student attitudes. Thus we would desire, as they may be available in your records, the instructor's age, sex, university degrees, years of teaching experience, and some measure of his research contributions. We should like to assume that the college administration would permit the acquisition of such data from the records by regular college employees in the office concerned. This will take some of the financial load from our shoulders and insure transcription of your records by persons cognizant with them. We shall, of course, indicate the form of transcription which will be most useful.

In our plan all data should be collected and in our hands by the 20th of May. We believe that we can provide evaluation profiles to each faculty member concerned before the conclusion of the first semester of the academic year 1947–1948, and quite likely before the end of November. The more intensive analysis of factors associated with the evaluations will possibly take longer to complete.

It should be our mutual understanding that any reports or evaluations which we make with respect to individual instructors will be held as confidential by the Rutgers office, and divulged only to the instructor concerned. We wish a clear understanding, both between ourselves and with faculty and student, that these personal ratings are for the sole use of the instructor himself. We feel that such a basis for the project is not only desirable in itself but will also constitute an important consideration in obtaining full and frank reports from the students. On the other hand, summary presentations shall not be treated as confidential. Thus, along with individual evaluations we shall prepare for non-confidential use a summary, average, profile of the faculty at large on the individual points of evaluation. Administrative usefulness can undoubtedly be made of such averages, particularly when comparative positions of different segments of the faculty are also shown; i.e., differences in types of evaluation by college division and, if feasible, by department.

It is our understanding that we may freely publish the results of this research, insofar as we do not expose individual instructors. It is assumed that the products of such analysis, whether or not published, will be made available to the administration of Brooklyn College.

We sincerely believe that this project is a worthwhile one both from the standpoint of scientific inquiry into an important field of human relations, and also as an aid in improvement of teaching. Obviously its successful conclusion must rest first of all upon the close cooperation of Brooklyn College, officers, faculty, and students. Without the wholehearted and enthusiastic support of each link of this chain, no amount of statistical effort will suffice. Clearly it must rest with you to insure such cooperation at the college, and just as clearly it must rest with us to bring out of this labor something of real significance to instructor and administrator—and perhaps most of all to the student.

The Survey Gets Under Way. Near the end of the academic year 1946–1947, the Student Reaction Survey was administered on the Brooklyn College campus. Not the least important part was that played by the Dean of Studies in publicizing the survey and arranging for its distribution. Following is an excerpt from an article subsequently prepared at Brooklyn and published in *School and Society*, describing in some detail the machinery for administering the survey:

The administration of the survey on the Brooklyn College campus was the responsibility of the Dean of Studies who arranged for the distribution, collection, and shipment of all questionnaire material to Rutgers University. The collection of this material for purposes of transmittal to the investigators at Rutgers University was done simply. Space was provided at Brooklyn College in the Office of the Dean of Studies where a large receptacle was placed so that students could easily deposit their completed questionnaires in sealed envelopes provided for that purpose. Student assistants, on a voluntary basis, saw to it that all material was returned in the sealed envelope, that it was tied in bundles, and that it was immediately shipped to Rutgers University. Despite extensive efforts to convince the student that for him this was an anonymous enterprise, at times it was necessary to reassure a timid student that his ballot was secret and that he need fear no reprisals. For the most part, however, students accepted the guarantees of the Rutgers investigators, of the Brooklyn College administration, and of the student members of the Faculty-Student Committee working on this project, and eagerly filed their completed questionnaires. A general reminder, circulated in all classes, brought in the returns of students who usually need this bit of additional prompting to fulfill an obligation.

The total of 6681 responses, representing more than ninety percent of the entire student body canvassed in the survey, may be attributed to several external factors which were operative in addition to any possible inherent desire on the part of students to participate in such an investigation of teaching competence. For one thing the study received proper presentation through student publicity channels with considerable emphasis on the precautionary measures devised to guarantee student anonymity. Another reason for the gratifying response was the fact that the questionnaire forms were carefully formulated and neatly printed so that they elicited the respect of the respondent.[1]

An even more precise picture of the system of distributing questionnaires can be obtained from the two notices reproduced below. The first, read to every student on campus, outlines the procedure for obtaining the survey materials; the second, distributed to student assistants, stresses the pains taken in assuring a complete sample.

Instructions on Distribution of
Student Reaction Survey

Dean of the Faculty
BROOKLYN COLLEGE
Brooklyn, N.Y.

May 14, 1947

To the Members
    of the
Teaching Staff.

Dear Colleague:

Please read this notice in all classes on Friday, May 16th and Monday, May 19th.

The Rutgers Survey for the rating of Brooklyn College teachers by their students will be conducted on the Brooklyn College campus during the week of May 19th. Material for the survey will be distributed outdoors on the College Quadrangle to each student currently enrolled in the day session. The distribution will take place on *Tuesday, May 20th*, between 10:00 A.M. and 4:00 P.M. If the weather does not permit an outdoor distribution on this day, the material will be distributed on the first fair day following. Students will pick up their material at the table carrying the initial letter of their last name: the men on the green near the front of the library; the women on the green near Bedford Avenue. All students are urged to pick up their envelope on the day of the outdoor distribution. Students who cannot obtain their material on that day may do so the following day in Room 2100 Boylan Hall.

The teacher rating forms are to be filled out in accordance with the instructions contained in them and returned *sealed* in the envelope provided for that purpose to Room 2117 Boylan or dropped in the

Rutgers Survey receptacle in the main lobby of Boylan Hall. *Please be sure to return the teacher rating forms as soon as possible,* but in no case later than *Monday, May 26th.* In order that the survey may yield a valuable study, all students are required to file a return by that date.

And the systematic detail which was necessary even with respect to such an apparently minor operation as the distribution of the questionnaires is shown in the notice which was sent to the corps of students who had volunteered to help.

INSTRUCTIONS TO STUDENTS DISTRIBUTING TEACHER RATING MATERIAL

Assignment: Time—   Place—
Date: Tuesday, May 20th, if the weather is fair. If not, on the first fair day following.
Place: The College Quadrangle

1. Report promptly at the time and to the table assigned to you. If you cannot do so for some reason, provide an alternate who will take over for you.
2. Do not, *under any circumstances,* leave your table. If you have covered the period for which you volunteered your services and your replacement has not reported to you, do the following:
   Either a) Call the staff member in charge of your division—he will be present on the green.
   or   b) Take your tray to the adjacent table and move the letter of your table (A, B, C, etc.) to that table.
3. As the student comes to your table, ask him for his name. Pick his envelope out of the file and hand it to him. *Be sure to get both first and last name.*
4. If an envelope for a student is not in the file check a few envelopes ahead or back for the one for which you are looking. (It may be out of alphabetical order.) If you cannot find it, refer the student to Mr. Goodhartz in Room 2109 Boylan the following day. Remember, there should be an envelope for every regularly enrolled day session student. *There are no envelopes for evening session students or students registered in the Veterans Session.*
5. Exercise care in the use of College equipment, such as files, tables, etc. Much of it is borrowed from various departments.
6. Avoid any controversies with individual students. Students with complaints are to be referred to Mr. Goodhartz, Room 2109 Boylan.

As representatives for the Rutgers Survey, you are expected to be
courteous and helpful.

7. Remember that the College deeply appreciates your services.

As a result of such careful planning, the completed questionnaires were collected (in sealed envelopes to guarantee their anonymity) on schedule and shipped to the Rutgers office, the small
balance of noncollectible questionnaires being accounted for primarily by reasons of absence or sickness.

Analysis and Reporting. The following six to eight months were
devoted to an analysis of the materials. A description of the methods
used, together with the questionnaire forms, will be given in the
next chapter, but it may be pointed out that even the simplest
handling of the data called for nearly forty thousand IBM cards,
to say nothing of the thousands of calculations required in comput-
ing the necessary "scores" and percentages.

Within six months after the administration of the survey, confidential individual ratings were mailed directly to the homes of
the 391 faculty members (see Chapter 5 for the forms used) and
shortly thereafter an over-all analysis of a nonconfidential nature
was submitted to the entire college community (see Chapters 6–
9). The entire process of analysis and reporting, in short, con-
sumed the better part of one academic year.

Faculty Reactions. After the confidential reports had been in the
hands of the individual faculty members for over a semester, the
Rutgers office sent a letter to each recipient asking for reactions
and comments. The results of this follow-up constitute, to date,
the most complete account of the "effects" of the project. These
details, with special reference to the whole question of the relationship between the project and the improvement of teaching,
are presented in Chapter 10.

In addition, certain formal reactions may be reported. The
President of the College had asked that each department devote at
least one meeting to a discussion of the project, and on the basis

of these discussions a subsequent memorandum was prepared by the President.

Aside from the value the student ratings may have had for the individual instructor, the departments will undoubtedly find important material for their discussions of, and efforts toward, the improvement of teaching, especially in the chapter entitled "The Relationship Between the Ideal and the Actual."

I think it can be argued that the survey served its purpose simply because of the professional discussion it has provoked on the campus, but a number of the specific conclusions certainly deserve further attention. No commitment has been made by the college as to further action, or concerning improvement of the survey methods and possible repetition of the whole process from time to time. Specific conclusions can be drawn in departments where they may be deemed appropriate but it is the responsibility of the Faculty Committee on Student Evaluation of Teachers to make recommendations to the Faculty as to the advisability of continuing the practice of student ratings of teachers, or the presentation of any other conclusions that may have a bearing on college practice as a whole.

Finally, as further evidence of our contention that the research itself constitutes only a segment of such a project, the President recently wrote to the sponsoring foundation:

From our point of view the project has served an extremely useful purpose in developing a sharpened interest in the improvement of teaching. The results of the survey constitute the starting point for further investigation of the problem by our Faculty Committee on Student Evaluation of Teachers which will, in all probability, submit proposals for faculty consideration.

Clearly, even the most experimental efforts with student evaluations require the cooperation of many groups, and a type of open-mindedness which permits the results to be, at least potentially, of long run value and significance.

After a consideration of the methodological problems, we shall, consequently, turn our attention to some of the specific research findings from the project and to the implications which they hold for the general problem of student-teacher relations.

5

The Question of Procedure:
One Possible Device

THE various attributes upon which professors may be judged or evaluated are, as Chapter 3 has indicated, of considerable range in their significance for the teaching process. Undoubtedly the confusion over the proper ends of college education has rendered, in many instances, student judgments of teachers of dubious value. It is difficult to achieve a standard by which student judgments themselves may be evaluated. If no superior judge may sit upon the professor's case, and if the student has some unknown degree of error in his estimate of professional skills, then the professor is obligated, by virtue of this very freedom, to learn how the student receives his presence. The central problem, then, is to articulate a series of teaching attributes which, when reported upon by his students, will give the professor this kind of information and insight.

Selecting the Attributes. This, in fact, must be the objective regardless of how one defines the goals of the professor. For example, no educator, professor or literate layman would equate speaking ability with knowledge of the subject, yet both, by any standard of modern education, are important elements inherent in the professor's role. The objective of the scale constructor is to sample as adequately as possible, within the limits of time and money, the total range of elements entering into effective instruction. High specificity is usually impossible since the very objectives and definition of "effective" instruction are elastic and subject also to a variety of opinions. Thus we could not permit ourselves to prejudge the professor by attempting to measure his attainment of certain ends of the classroom which we as educators or which other researchers might arbitrarily deem desirable. Rather our approach was to break the professorial role into component elements upon which any generally accepted concept of the teaching function must stand. For these purposes the teaching role may be conceived as the counterpart of learning in such a way that it may be grasped by the student and stimulate his further rational thinking in the field at hand. This is clearly a minimum definition, taking no account of the social responsibilities and character building functions of the classroom situation which are too diffuse in their meanings, techniques and effects to be measured in this type of inquiry.

On this basis, and with these qualifications, we have drawn heavily upon the earlier research, but have gone one step further in attempting to construct a theoretical framework within which various traits or attributes would have their own logic. Thus three general types of attributes may be theoretically postulated to subsume all professorial characteristics relevant to the performance of the teaching role. These may be stated briefly as 1) subject matter competence or learning; 2) pedagogical (mainly communicative) skills; and 3) attributes of personality. The first of these includes the professor in relationship to his subject, his competence as the "man of learning." The second relates to the instructional skills whereby the professor utilizes his learning toward the goals of instruction: stimulation of thinking, clear presentation of data, etc. The third is the residual "human" element, the personality factors which frame and color the expressions of skills and learning.

This mode of approach is strictly an analytical one. Few actual manifestations of professorial behavior are readily classifiable *in toto* into one or another of these categories. However, it is imperative that these different elements be recognized if an adequate sampling of the vital instructional characteristics is to be had. Obviously no brief questionnaire will tap extensively each of the categories, but if any over-all evaluation of the instructor is to be derived, students must express themselves on traits relevant to each of these major areas of competence. With this theoretical construct in mind, the actual selection of traits included in this inquiry came through several processes. The literature of teacher evaluations was studied closely with particular attention to suggestive questions in the various phases we sought to test. Save for personal appearance, a sense of humor, and moral character—items which have frequently appeared in earlier studies—we have included all other traits upon which there has been any marked degree of consensus. Free or unstructured interviews were also held with students in order to gain insight into the character and content of their thinking. These unprompted responses provided many clews which were then examined further for relevance. In addition, other attributes of instruction were supplied introspectively as the result of personal observations in the college classroom both as students and as teachers. From these efforts perhaps fifty "ideal" or "deplorable" instructional characteristics were derived and grouped by their functional similarities—whether they pertained to learning, to conversation techniques, or to personality.

Furthermore, mainly for assessing the relative importance of the traits, another introspective device was utilized. Each member of the research group selected from his own experience his "best" and his "worst" college teacher and proceeded to list the traits which in his judgment were most vital in the "best" and most deplorable in the "worst." [1] Such a process proved particularly useful in opening our eyes to the disutility of many alleged "ideal" traits on our extensive list. Classroom mannerisms, for example, although frequently noted in professorial images, have no place within such a theoretical framework. [2] Such explorations as these assured us that no wide gaps remained in our theoretic construction of the professorial role for which we had a more or less concrete working formulation.

To meet space and time requirements it was further necessary to narrow the number of our specific attributes while maintaining the desired range of coverage. This was accomplished mainly through the actual intensive questioning of students.[3] Attributes elicited from them in accounting for "why" Professor X was "good" or "bad" substantiated the meaningfulness of certain items, and in some instances modified the form of expression.

Through these processes the ten attributes as shown on pages 55–56 were selected for inclusion on the questionnaire.

The justification of this artificial fragmentation of a whole is to render to the student each of these instructional elements in sufficiently specific form as to permit evaluation. Obviously the more or less tangible traits which students see in their professors do not fit neatly into such abstract pigeon holes, but one or more of the elements are manifest in any given attribute. Thus, students are assumed to feel that they have some knowledge of the professor's competence as such, and that this can probably be visualized by them as a simple unitary characteristic. In the realm of communication skills, specificity is called for, and in a brief questionnaire few phases can be explored. Speaking ability is the only trait utilized involving virtually pure technique. In the field of personality it is obviously impossible to include all relevant impressions a student might gain. However, the instructor's attitude toward the student is of critical importance and is included, as is the total effect of the professor, in terms of human warmth and likableness. Actually many of the most critical measures of instruction are heterogeneous. Thus encouragement to thinking may be thought of as a manifestation of intellectual, communicative and personality factors. Tolerance to disagreement rests but slightly within the area of knowledge, but strongly in the personality pattern and in the professor's personal definition of the communication process. Enthusiasm toward subject is most clearly a personality factor but with a dependence upon scholarship rather than upon pedagogical technique. Organization of materials and explanatory ability are clearly communicative techniques but rooted as well in subject matter competence. In short, while no simple schematic presentation can adequately reflect the close interdependence of the complex bases of professional ability, these approximations may assist in classification.

Constructing the Rating Scale. In any survey designed to allow expression of opinion by a large student body, and further calculated to yield *comparable* data for each faculty member concerned, spontaneous comments by each student obviously cannot be relied upon exclusively. While such qualitative observations would be useful for some forms of intensive analysis, they are methodologically not feasible in any extensive inquiry. Consequently, as in other systematic approaches to faculty evaluation, a rating scale was devised, applicable to each of the selected characteristics. Thus on the trait of *tolerance to disagreement* the following four levels were provided with instructions that the student should check the level most clearly applicable:

Encourages and values reasonable disagreement
Accepts disagreement fairly well
Discourages disagreement
Dogmatic, intolerant of disagreement

The fact that four levels of response were available precluded, of course, any clustering at a mid-point in the scale. The specification of each level, rather than allowing the student to give an undirected response to a statement of deviation from an average, has distinct advantages. First of all we did not wish to set ratings upon a comparative basis, i.e., Professor X as compared with Professor Z. Use of the term "average" was avoided since its semantic effect is comparative, whereas the term "satisfactory" is less so. The process of pre-testing offered firm conviction that students in general have absorbed and apply standards which in their own minds are absolute—although they may well have been derived through a process of comparative evaluation beginning long before college entrance. It was thus believed that an absolute scale should be implied since it corresponded to tendencies in student thinking.[4] A second advantage is that it permits closer control of what was meant in the statement of the trait. Thus in the case of speaking ability we are not concerned with standards in quite the same sense as is the judge of a speech contest. We are interested in speaking ability as a factor in effective teaching. Accordingly we may offer a highest score to a teacher specified as "skilled in presenting materials, voice and presence excellent." But a man with a definite speech defection in a technical sense *could* achieve the next highest rating "adequate, *does not detract from course*." Our procedure in general was designed to permit the narrowing of standards to fit the classroom situation and its demands.

In detail the characteristics with their respective scales developed as follows:

1. *Organization of Subject Matter*
   Systematic and thoroughly organized
   Adequate, could be better
   Inadequate organization detracts from course
   Confused and unsystematic

2. *Speaking Ability*
   Skilled in presenting material, voice and presence excellent
   Adequate, does not detract from course
   Poor speaker, detracts from course
   Poor speaking techniques serious handicap in course

3. *Ability to Explain*
   Explanations clear and to point
   Explanations usually adequate
   Explanations often inadequate
   Explanations seldom given or usually inadequate

4. *Encouragement to Thinking*
   Has great ability to make you think for yourself
   Considerable stimulation to thinking
   Not much stimulus to thinking
   Discouraging to thought

5. *Attitude Toward Students*

Sympathetic, helpful, actively concerned
Moderately sympathetic
Routine in attitude—avoids individual contact
Distant, aloof, cold

6. *Knowledge of Subject*

Exceedingly well informed in field of course
Adequately informed
Not well informed
Very inadequately informed

7. *Attitude Toward Subject*

Enthusiastic, enjoys teaching
Rather interested
Rather bored—routine interest
Not interested, disillusioned with subject

8. *Fairness in Examinations*

Testing excellently done
Testing is satisfactory
Testing sometimes unfair
Testing mostly unfair

9. *Tolerance to Disagreement*

Encourages and values reasonable disagreement
Accepts disagreement fairly well
Discourages disagreement
Dogmatic, intolerant of disagreement

10. *Instructor as "Human Being"*

Attractive personality, would like to know him
Satisfactory personality
Rather unattractive personality
Not the kind of person you care for

Under each characteristic the student was asked to indicate the degree of satisfaction he found. This was accomplished by the four evaluative statements, ranging in effect from "excellent" to "seriously inadequate." Since any study of attitudes rests ultimately upon the adequacy of the questionnaire, the methodology employed here is of crucial concern.

The rating scale used here assumes degrees of student attitudes ranging from quantitative abundance to a quantitative lack in respect to each trait. This implies that the standards used by students is roughly the same for all. It should not be assumed, however, that each trait is in fact, or in the student's mind, equal in importance. Thus the separate items on the scale may ask for student attitudes on traits of trivial as well as basic importance for effective instruction. This in no way diminishes the validity of the technique, but rather calls for careful interpretation. Thus a professor's scores on individual items are not additive. We would not be dealing with an "average" professor just because he scored very high on stimulation to thinking but equally low on public speaking ability: one does not serve to cancel out the other. Not only is it essential that the importance of the trait itself to the educational process be considered, it is essential that we know the importance of the trait to the student himself. Thus, if a professor is to gain maximum insight from the student evaluation he must also know how the student evaluates that trait.

A Measuring Rod: the Student's Ideal Construct. An integral complement to the rating scale itself has been the student's expression of instructional ideals. This was gained by providing a list of ideal traits, corresponding identically with the list of attributes on which actual instructors were evaluated. Here, however, and prior to the actual evaluations, the student was asked to select the three attributes which, in his judgment, were most important for an effective professor in each of several fields of study. While educators may or may not agree with the Brooklyn College students in their characterizations of the "ideal teacher," such data are essential for full comprehension of the professorial image. Without such a yardstick the full significance of the rating on any attribute is lost, for we would not know whether or not the attribute itself held high value for the student. This point takes on added meaning to the individual instructor who studies his own evaluation when we recall that some attributes are undoubtedly "competitive" with others. Thus if organization is wittingly sacrificed for the sake of stimulating insights generated in the classroom, the professor may find it useful to know the significance attached to each of these partially competing attributes. While student judgments cannot be viewed as proper determinants of professorial decisions, knowledge of those judgments may be used to forestall unnecessary tensions.

Other Factors Influencing Student Judgments. The significance of the scale likewise varies with factors external to the professor. Where a single system of ratings is applied to diverse faculties it is clear that within the total range of relevant traits certain of them apply more critically or more intensively to instruction in some divisions than to others. On an intensive study basis it is perhaps feasible to adapt scaling techniques to individual departments and their peculiar problems of instruction. This, however, is not feasible where the end is to secure results comparable between departments or divisions, since analysis is all but precluded on any but a departmental basis. Such exactitude in applicability is not essential methodologically. In this study a standard questionnaire was used regardless of the area of instruction and regardless of the type of course. This does not assume in any way that any given attribute has equal relevance under all circumstances of instruction. Thus in the teaching of language, professorial tolerance to disagreement is relevant on a far less extensive basis than would be true for the humanities or social sciences. Tolerance to disagreement is not irrelevant to the language professor; rather the range of tolerance is more confined and its meaning may tend more toward "reasonableness in attitude toward student error" than toward the admission of free play in value judgment. The very fact that the range of tolerance is low in certain fields does not make the student evaluation any less valid, although it may have less over-all importance.

Similarly classroom conditions beyond the control of the professor or the student might well influence or "explain" the ratings given the professor. Class size, for example, must be taken into account if interpretations are to be adequate.

It is obvious that no student body will be homogeneous in its judgments of a faculty. In order that the ratings have maximum meaning, various segments of the student body are compared. Thus we may test the influence of sex, age and other differences as well as the effect of "grades" upon the professorial image.

Thus within the limits of this type of statistical inquiry we have attempted to sample the range and depth of student attitudes toward their professors. Beyond this an effort has been made to place these evaluations in a context of student thinking regarding valuable attributes in the ideal professor. A student-created yardstick is thus provided for measuring the stature of the professor's image. Beyond this, we have tried to analyze the major factors thought to be of possible relevance in influencing student judgment.

A replica of the questionnaire used in the study can be found in the appendix.

Reporting the Results. The questionnaire, as can readily be seen, provides for complete coverage of the faculty; each student to evaluate as many as five of his current instructors. Anything less was considered inadequate for the purpose of giving to the individual instructor an accurate picture of his effect on his audience. Equally essential for implementing this primary objective of the study was to allow each instructor the opportunity—insofar as this was possible without violating any confidences—to see himself in relation to other members of the faculty. Obviously, only in relation to some norm do the ratings become meaningful. In this case, average performance of teachers in a general area of instruction, i.e., arts, sciences, social sciences, was selected as the standard for comparison. Departmental averages were deemed too revealing, particularly in the smaller departments.

Before constructing averages, however, some method had to be devised for scoring the student evaluations. Each evaluation, corresponding to each page of Form B of the questionnaire, had been transferred to an IBM punch card and the distribution of student reactions for each instructor tabulated, as in the following illustration:

STUDENT EVALUATIONS
PROFESSOR X

1. *Organization of subject matter*

Systematic and thoroughly organized	23%
Adequate, could be better	51
Inadequate organization detracts from course	15
Confused and unsystematic	8
No answer	3

2. *Speaking Ability*

Skilled in presenting material, voice and presence excellent	34%
Adequate, does not detract from course	33
Poor speaker, detracts from course	23
Poor speaking techniques serious handicap in course	10
No answer	—

For purposes of simplification and of comparability, a single index number or score was calculated from these percentage distributions of student reactions to each professor on the ten criteria. Weights of 3 to 0 were arbitrarily assigned to the four points on the scales ranging roughly from "excellent" to "poor." Thus, Professor X, in organization of subject matter, received a total of 186 points. Since the greatest number of points attainable was 300, the total was divided by 3, in order to reduce the figure to the familiar 0 to 100 range. Professor X, then, dividing 186 by 3, received a score of 62 in organization. His score on speaking ability was 64.

The Individual Reports. The problem of providing a standard against which the professor might assess his own performance was resolved by furnishing quartile position scores of professors in the arts, sciences and social sciences. In the appropriate quartile position for his general area of instruction were recorded the professor's actual scores. These appear in italics in the example shown below. Professor X, an arts instructor, can see at a glance that on six attributes of good teaching, he was judged as good as the top 50 per cent of all arts instructors, that he fell slightly below the average in explanatory ability and in personality, and that his organization of course materials and speaking ability are as bad as the lowest 25 per cent of all arts instructors. In addition to the details of the rating sheet itself, the professor was presented with some "findings relevant to the interpretation of the ratings." From these, Professor X can draw little consolation, unless his classes are composed of an unusually large number of poor students, who tend to apply somewhat more rigorous standards than better students in evaluating their teachers. A sample of the individual reports as they were sent to each faculty member follows:

12/8/47

STUDENT REACTION SURVEY
Brooklyn College

Dept. of Sociology
Rutgers University

A NOTE ON THE INDIVIDUAL INSTRUCTOR'S RATING

You have been rated by a large sample of your students on each of ten attributes important to the teacher at the college level. (The samples were drawn at random and typically include from two-thirds to four-fifths of any instructor's students.) The charts on the attached page show your rating on each of these attributes in comparison with the *average* and the distribution of ratings given to the entire Brooklyn College faculty classified by academic area. Your score on each quality represents an index number computed from the ratings given you by your students. Thus a score of 100 would indicate that all of your students had rated you as "excellent" on that particular quality; a score of zero would indicate that all students rated you as inadequate or unsatisfactory. (The students were given an appropriately-worded four-point scale for each attribute ranging in a semantic sense from "excellent" to "inadequate.") Very few ratings, in fact, approximate these extremes, and of course any score is most meaningful when taken in comparison with the scores of your colleagues.

It should be emphasized again that these individual scores are completely confidential. Even here at the Rutgers office your ratings during the machine tabulation and calculating process have been designated by a code number. Only for the purposes of mailing has your name been attached. The Rutgers group also wishes to point out its cognizance of the fact that student opinion is not the only criterion of "good teaching." Within the scope of the survey, however, it is the only one which we have attempted to measure.

How to Read the Ratings

1. You need be concerned only with that part of each scale which pertains to your general area of instruction; i.e., the arts, physical or natural sciences, social sciences. The number written in red on each scale represents your score for the particular quality.

2. The solid line drawn horizontally across the mid-point of each scale indicates the average (median) score for all teachers, and the dotted lines on either side of the median mark off the first and third quartiles. The top and bottom figures on each scale designate the actual range of the scores.

3. Thus, if your score is in the fourth quartile, you are among the highest 25% of all teachers in your area. If your score is in the first quartile you are among the lowest 25%, etc.

Findings Relevant to the Interpretation of the Ratings

Although the over-all analysis of the material from this survey is not yet complete, some of the inter-relationships which have emerged to date are relevant to a basic understanding of the individual ratings.

1. *Size of class*. On most attributes, size of class is not significantly related to student evaluations. There are, however, some interesting exceptions. For example, students in small (under 20) social science classes rate the instructors higher in their ability to stimulate thought and in their tolerance to disagreement. Natural science students report relatively little encouragement to thought in the large class situation (40 or more), but interestingly enough science teachers of large classes are more highly praised both for their knowledge of the subject and their organization of the materials.

2. *Required vs. elective courses*. In the arts, whether a course is taken as required or as elective makes little difference in student evaluation. But in the sciences there is a tendency for students taking re-

quired courses to rate their instructor higher than in the case of those taking elective courses. In contrast, in the social sciences, higher ratings are more often given by those taking the courses as electives.

3. *Scholarship*. Within all three academic areas, and on all of the teaching attributes under consideration, students of low scholastic standing rate their instructors more rigorously than those with a relatively high academic average. With respect to "encouragement to thinking" and "fairness in examinations," all students tend to record dissatisfaction in the form of critical ratings.

Other Findings of General Interest

While the generalized findings must wait upon the completion of the larger analysis, several observations on the score distributions themselves are currently pertinent. It is clear, for instance, that all students agree that the faculty excells in one attribute—knowledge of subject. Perhaps no greater tribute could have been paid to the faculty at large. On the other hand, there is, relatively speaking, a consistently poor opinion of the faculty on "encouragement to thinking." The discrepancy in student estimates between these two important attributes would seem to constitute a problem worthy of careful consideration. The other attribute upon which critical ratings were recorded—"fairness in examinations"—is somewhat more mechanical in nature and thus perhaps more easily approached.

Finally, the ratings are surprisingly consistent when the three academic areas are compared. The one outstanding difference is the relatively high estimate of social science instructors on "tolerance to disagreement."

Instructor's Rating   Professor X

ORGANIZATION OF SUBJECT MATTER				KNOWLEDGE OF SUBJECT		
Arts	*Science*	*Soc. Sci.*		*Arts*	*Science*	*Soc. Sci.*
99	98	99	4th Quartile	100 [92]	100	100
88	88	90	3rd Quartile	94	94	95
77	79	78	2nd Quartile	90	87	89
64 [62]	68	61	1st Quartile	83	76	81
16	27	25		55	44	58

SPEAKING ABILITY

Arts	Science	Soc. Sci.	
99	97	98	
			4th Quartile
89	82	85	
			3rd Quartile
78	70	72	
			2nd Quartile
66	62	59	
[64]			1st Quartile
36	31	21	

ATTITUDE TOWARD SUBJECT

Arts	Science	Soc. Sci.
99	98	99
89	86	91
[84]		
78	75	82
67	64	71
36	35	41

ABILITY TO EXPLAIN

Arts	Science	Soc. Sci.	
96	97	97	
			4th Quartile
82	82	84	
			3rd Quartile
75	72	77	
[68]			2nd Quartile
63	57	58	
			1st Quartile
38	24	34	

FAIRNESS IN EXAMINATIONS

Arts	Science	Soc. Sci.
88	90	88
73	73	72
[69]		
68	64	63
56	55	58
24	24	37

ENCOURAGEMENT TO THINKING

Arts	Science	Soc. Sci.	
95	89	93	
			4th Quartile
68	68	73	
[67]			3rd Quartile
58	61	62	
			2nd Quartile
49	50	53	
			1st Quartile
30	33	30	

TOLERANCE TO DISAGREEMENT

Arts	Science	Soc. Sci.
98	93	97
80	80	87
[74]		
72	70	81
60	59	67
22	30	42

ATTITUDE TOWARD STUDENTS				PERSONALITY		
Arts	Science	Soc. Sci.		Arts	Science	Soc. Sci.
100 ----- 99 ----- 98			------------------	96 ----	95 ----	98
			4th Quartile			
84 ----- 82 ----- 84			------------------	84 ----	84 ----	85
81			3rd Quartile			
73 ——— 72 ——— 74			———————————	74 ———	75 ———	77
			2nd Quartile	69		
58 ----- 61 ----- 65			------------------	61 ----	62 ----	65
			1st Quartile			
25 ----- 28 ----- 25			------------------	27 ----	29 ----	35

Before leaving the professor and at the risk of repetition, it should be emphasized again that in the final analysis it is only Professor X who can interpret his scores, only he who can judge to what extent this mandate from his students should be heeded. It was also suggested earlier in this chapter that the ten criteria selected for evaluation are by no means equally important and that they must necessarily vary in relative importance from one subject matter field to another. It may be added that specific goals of instruction also vary from one professor to another and that these, too, must be taken into account in determining what course of action to pursue on the basis of such student reactions. An interesting illustration in this connection is the case of a social science instructor (see Chapter 10) whose students judged him low on organization of subject matter. This was interpreted by the instructor as a failure on his part to clarify the objectives of the course; his decision, therefore, was not to attempt an improvement in subject matter organization but to strive for a better understanding in the classroom of what it was he hoped to accomplish. Similarly, there is the case of a speech teacher whose low rating on organization arose as a result of close individual supervision in the classroom, a system of instruction which precludes strict adherence to a tightly organized outline. Numerous classroom situations could be cited in which one or more teaching attributes are consciously and legitimately sacrificed in order that the students may derive other values. It is, therefore, not the intention of the present authors to recommend to the individual instructor that he aim merely for perfect scores. The speech teacher referred to above, who gave up what he felt was an effective method of instruction in order to achieve a higher score on organization, was misusing the information of the rating sheet. Student evaluations are, from various points of view, highly personal information. The scores belong to the individual instructor; their interpretation and action based upon them belong to him alone.

Over-all Analysis. At the time the individual reports were submitted to the faculty, little progress had been made on the analysis of the student ratings as a whole and their relationship to some of the data called for on Form A of the questionnaire. While the individual confidential reports were continually the main focus of the study, a secondary objective was the over-all analysis of a representative sample of student ratings, with an eye to understanding the influence on the ratings of such factors as the student's age, sex, and field of interest as well as his general attitudes and opinions toward college. Of the five instructors rated by each student, the first one was to become part of the sample for intensive study. It was with respect to this first evaluation that special care had to be taken. To allow the student to rate his five instructors in whatever order he pleased would be to risk a variety of biases. Students might be expected to select for first consideration the professor they liked best, or the one they liked least. They might tend to select the professor whom they had seen most recently, or the one they met most frequently. The sources of bias in this kind of free selection are unpredictable, with no guarantee that the errors will cancel out.

On the theory that no biasing influence is exerted by the alphabetical listing of students' names, the method for selecting a random sample of ratings, described on page 3 of Form A of the questionnaire, was devised. The student body was divided into five groups determined by the first letter of the student's last name. Each group was assigned a particular instructor to rate on Form

A, depending upon the order of his classes. Thus, students whose names began with letters A-E rated the instructor with whom they met first during the week; those whose last initials were F-H rated the instructor whom they met second during the week, and so on until all five instructors, which each student typically meets during a normal week, were accounted for.

This rating, together with the remaining responses to Form A of the questionnaire, were punched on an IBM card. By this method, comparisons were possible between a student's evaluation of his professor and various descriptive data, both about the course itself and about the student evaluator. Thus, such influences as maturity of the rater, his scholarly ability, his general attitude toward college could be matched against his judgment of the instructor. Above all, it became possible to stand a real professor up against the measuring rod of the student's ideal. The details of this analysis are presented in Chapters 6, 7, and 8.

Perhaps some mention should be made of items 11, 12, and 13 on the evaluation sheet, which call for an over-all rating of the instructor "compared to all instructors you have had," and ask the student to point out the "greatest weakness" and the "strongest asset" of the instructor under consideration, in terms of the ten categories. In general, these items did not appear to add anything to the picture. While they did serve as an additional check on the reliability of the ratings, the information they elicited was easily obtained from the preceding ten items.

Still another analytic procedure remains to be discussed. This is in connection with the other side of the teacher-student relationship. Having studied the relationship between various student characteristics and the ratings of professors, it was only logical to proceed to a similar analysis of various professorial characteristics. For this purpose, information about each professor—age, sex, marital status, academic rank, degrees, publications, membership in professional societies, etc.—was collected from the administrative files of the College. These data, in turn, were punched on an IBM card, together with the professor's quartile position in each of the ten criteria of good teaching, transferred from the confidential rating sheet. These results are discussed in Chapter 9 under the heading of "Who Are the Good Teachers?"

There remains only the data presented in Chapter 10 concerning teacher reactions to the student ratings. These materials were obtained by means of a follow-up letter and topical questionnaire, and were treated qualitatively, with no attempt to apply statistical techniques. In a sense, these are a series of case histories. They tell the story of how the insights gleaned from these ratings were interpreted and carried back into the classroom. From this point of view, the utility of any program of student ratings must ultimately be determined on the basis of such testimony.

In conclusion, this chapter has described in some detail the development of a research "instrument" for use in obtaining a systematic picture of students' conception of a faculty. We have also indicated how the results so obtained were handled and analyzed. We entertain, however, no belief that either the technique or the procedure are perfect, or necessarily the best that might be devised. We are, rather, primarily concerned with the implications which research of this type holds for one of the problems of higher education, and since the justification for this interest springs from a detailed experience on one college campus, we turn now to some of the specific findings.

6

What the Student Wants

IF the student is to be given some systematic opportunity to evaluate his professor, he must at the same time be allowed to express his ideal expectations of the professional function. For one without the other becomes only a half statement and may be quite meaningless. There is, for example, one conclusion to be drawn from a student who is critical of a professor who has failed to give what the student most wanted, i.e., stimulation to individual thinking; but quite a different conclusion is demanded if the student expressed little regard for this pedagogical result but rather had pinned his hopes on "learning the subject matter." And either of these conclusions would have been impossible to derive if no provision had been made for an expression of the ideal. The professor would have been judged critically, but in the latter case far less seriously than in the former.

This chapter, consequently, reports on students' expectations since they, in this sense, set the stage for the actual ratings. The relationship between the two, the ideal versus the actual, will then be subsequently analyzed in detail.

The precise role of a college instructor in the classroom situation depends upon his personality and value judgments, and to some extent also upon the nature of the course taught. It is obvious, for example, that instructors vary markedly in the degree to which their emphasis is upon presentation of concrete factual materials or to what degree it is upon the stimulation of thinking and the handling of ideas by the students. (There is, of course, no implication here that these are mutually exclusive categories.) From a slightly different angle, instructors vary in the extent to which they permit personal value judgments and personal choices between debatable alternatives to become evident to their students.

In an attempt to throw some light upon students' attitudes and expectations toward broadly different approaches to teaching, these two sets of instructional methods were specifically posed and student reaction to each was sought: stimulation versus factualness, and objectivity versus personal judgments.

It should be evident that an instructor's tendencies in respect to these different approaches is not simply a matter of personal taste or attitude. Different types of courses probably demand different types and levels of factualness, and of thought stimulation. Likewise different types of courses may vary in the degree to which personal judgments of the instructor are relevant. On the assumption that such situational factors are fairly homogeneous within each major segment of the curriculum, student expressions of attitude were obtained separately for "the arts," "social sciences," and the "natural sciences." [1]

While this device does not hold constant such factors as differences in course level, and to some extent overlooks known differences in the nature of courses within a single curriculum, these inexactnesses probably do not distort the student responses. And certainly they are of little significance for the comparison of attitudes in different segments of the student body. Our primary concern is not so much with precision in measurement as with gaining some rough indications of student valuation of certain basic methodological principles in instruction.

Facts versus Ideas. While it should be self-evident that there is no conflict, and in fact quite a complementary relationship, between facts and ideas, it is certain that instructors vary in their position on the continuum from the extreme of imparting only substantive knowledge to that of direct provocation, "needling" and generalizing. Which type of instructor do the students prefer—one who tends more to be a "presenter of facts," or one who is more clearly the "stimulator of ideas?"

The question asked was:

Two instructors have different approaches to teaching. Read their approaches, then answer a, b, and c.
  1. The first places emphasis on factual materials.
  2. The second places emphasis on ideas.
Which instructor would you prefer for a course dealing with:
  a. The arts?
  b. The physical and biological sciences?
  c. The social sciences?

Student attitudes on this question vary greatly, depending upon whether the hypothetical instructor is teaching in the sciences, the arts, or the social sciences.

In the arts, 85%

in the social sciences, 75%

and in the sciences, 13%

of the students would seek the instructor who placed emphasis on ideas.

The most significant variations in attitude toward instructional approach lie in student evaluations for the different academic fields. The student body is relatively homogeneous in its attitude toward instructional approach within each separate field. There are, however, a few interesting differences between some segments of the student population. For example, those of high scholastic standing are more favorable to instructors who stimulate thought and less favorable to factual presentations regardless of the field of the course. Home economics majors more frequently desire factual approaches in each field and engineers concur in respect to courses in the social sciences. There is also a slight tendency for advancement in academic status to be reflected in greater stress upon ideas and less upon factualness.

Although the great majority of all students prefer factual presentations in physical sciences and "stimulating" presentations in social sciences and arts, superior scholars are more favorable to thought stimulation than inferior scholars in *all* fields of study.

TABLE 2

PROPORTION OF STUDENTS FAVORING "IDEAS" ACCORDING TO SCHOLARSHIP LEVEL OF STUDENT

	Arts Teachers	Science Teachers	Social Science Teachers	(N)
Superior students *	87%	17%	77%	1525
Average students	85	13	75	3113
Poor students	81	11	72	1805
				6443 †

* Students receiving an average grade of "B" or better are designated "superior," those receiving "B—" or "C+" are called "average," while "poor" refers to all students whose average grade is "C" or less.
† Data on all-college grade average not available for 238 students.

There is also a fairly consistent tendency for advancement in college to reflect a desire for instructional emphasis upon ideas. This is true regardless of whether the course is arts, science, or social science. However, differences between successive class levels are not of statistical significance. Thus, for example, in attitudes toward instruction in the arts, the following proportions of students favor emphasis on ideas:

> 83% of the freshmen
> 84% of the sophomores
> 85% of the juniors
> 87% of the seniors

Except for majors in home economics, differences between curricular groups are not generally of significance. Among home economics majors there is widespread preference for factualness whether the course is in arts, science, or social science. Thus while three-fourths of all students prefer emphasis upon ideas in social sciences, only two-thirds of the home economists display such a conviction. A similar although slightly less pronounced difference occurs in respect to their attitudes regarding other areas of study. The only other curricular group showing any marked deviation from the norm is in the pre-engineering majors' attitude toward social sciences. Here the pre-engineers would seek factual instruction in preference to idea stimulation even more frequently than would the home economics majors. There is no evidence, however, that significant differences exist between the most populous curricular groups in their attitudes.

Other variables such as veteran status, sex, age, employment experience, and extracurricular activities appear to have little or no effect upon student attitudes toward this aspect of instruction.

Expression of Personal Judgments by the Instructor. It has long been a matter of debate as to whether instructors should inject into the classroom observations which are expressions of opinion, conviction or value judgment. This problem was presented to the students in terms of a choice between two instructors, one of whom made evident such value judgments, and the other who gave no evidence of value judgments in his teaching.[2]

The question put to the students on this issue was:

Two instructors differ in their personal participation in the course material. Read how they differ, then answer a, b, and c.
  1. The first makes classroom expression of personal opinions, convictions, value judgments, etc.
  2. The second gives no evidence in classroom of personal opinions, value judgments, etc.
Which instructor would you prefer for a course dealing with:
  a. The arts?
  b. The physical and biological sciences?
  c. The social sciences?

Student attitudes regarding expression of personal judgments are, as shown in Table 3, strikingly different depending upon the nature of the course. In courses dealing with social sciences or the arts, anywhere from two-thirds to four-fifths of the students wish to have personal judgments expressed, whereas in the physical and natural sciences a substantial majority favor no expression of personal judgments.

It is clear that in courses where value judgments and matters of conviction are most likely to arise, the student body in the main

TABLE 3

PROPORTION OF STUDENTS FAVORING EXPRESSION OF
PERSONAL OPINION BY ARTS, SCIENCE, AND
SOCIAL SCIENCE TEACHERS

Arts teachers	80%
Social science teachers	68
Science teachers	38

$$100\% = 6681$$

wishes no Olympian objectivity. The instructor in the arts or social sciences who attempts to cover up his personal views is not fulfilling most students' concept of a good teacher.

Different segments of the student body show little variation in their responses on this question. In some instances, as in the case of arts courses, scholastic standing of the student may have some effect upon attitude toward personal expressions. In this area, superior students show a slightly higher tendency to favor personal expression of viewpoint; however, this tendency is not manifest in regard to courses in other fields. Other variables fail to indicate even such a slight association. It is apparent that the student body is quite homogeneous in its viewpoint on this issue, insofar as we are able to determine. Our data are insufficiently detailed to gain any understanding of the types of students who fail to conform to the general attitude on instructor's expression of personal opinion.

Qualities of Good Teaching. In order to explore further the general nature of the student's construct of a "good teacher," the predetermined list of teaching attributes was provided as a list of positive qualities, for evaluation as to relative importance for effective teaching. Thus the student was asked to select the *three* items most important to good teaching in the arts, sciences and social sciences.

The question, as put, and the main results follow:

Here is a list of qualities important to good teaching. Read the list carefully, then answer questions a, b, and c.
Of these qualities which *three* would you consider to be of greatest importance in a course dealing with:
   a. The physical and biological sciences?
   b. The social sciences?
   c. The arts?

TABLE 4

QUALITIES THOUGHT TO BE IMPORTANT TO GOOD TEACHING

	Arts Teachers	Science Teachers	Soc. Sci. Teachers
Systematic organization of subject matter	32%	78%	48%
Good speaking ability	31	6	11
Ability to explain clearly	42	89	38
Ability to encourage thought	47	17	70
Sympathetic attitude toward students	9	5	3
Expert knowledge of subject	54	70	42
Enthusiastic attitude toward subject	46	16	26
Fairness in making and grading tests	8	10	7
Tolerance toward student disagreement	11	2	45
Pleasing personality	16	4	5

$$100\% = 6681$$

It is clear that the qualities essential for effective instruction vary considerably in the student's eyes, depending upon the type of course taught. Thus, the three most frequently chosen in each of the fields are:

Arts

Knowledge of subject	54%
Encourages thought	47
Enthusiastic	46

Sciences

Explanation	89%
Organization	78
Knowledge	70

Social Sciences

Encourages thought	70%
Organization	48
Tolerance to disagreement	45

The more rigorous attitude toward the sciences is readily apparent. Less than a fifth of the students specified the importance of encouragement to thought, or enthusiasm, for science teaching, whereas these were outstanding ideal traits of the arts instructor, and commonly desired ones in social sciences.

Most evident is the close agreement of the students on their three outstanding requirements for the science teacher. This instructional role is evidently most clearly visualized, or stereotyped, in student thinking. At the other extreme the ideal characterization of the arts teacher is not widely agreed upon; only in respect to knowledge of subject do more than one-half of the students concur on what are important attributes. While there is widespread agreement that the social science instructor should encourage thought, this is the only ideal trait which the majority of students believe to be among the top three in importance.

It is necessary, however, to consider not only those traits looked for in teachers, but also those presumably desirable traits to which very few students attach outstanding significance. It would appear that the less important traits in any one field also tend to be unimportant in the other fields. Thus, students very infrequently look upon the instructor's sympathetic attitude as being important. Likewise, fairness on tests was important to 10 per cent or less of the students, regardless of instructional field. A pleasing personality was demanded by 16 per cent of the students in regard to instructors in the arts, and was largely overlooked in other courses. Only in the arts was speaking ability a trait of some importance and only in social sciences was tolerance to disagreement a frequently selected outstanding trait. In this instance only was a quality widely believed to be important in one area considered of trivial value in the other two.

Variations in Conceptions of "Good Teaching." It is to be expected that individual differences in the students' backgrounds and experiences would be reflected in different evaluations of what constitutes good teaching. Such differences are, in fact, evidenced in some aspects of the student selection of ideal traits for each of the course areas. But perhaps more surprising is the relatively high degree of similarity in the judgments of different segments of the student body regarding ideal instructional traits. None of the variables studied reveals striking differences in the traits commonly judged most important. Although interesting differences arise in the proportion of students of different types selecting certain ideal traits, there is an over-all homogeneity in popular demand for certain attributes, depending upon the type of course given, but not upon student characteristics insofar as they are measured here.

The uniformity in attitude between different student groupings is most outstanding for courses in the sciences. Differences in sex, veteran status, scholarship, and all other measured variables fail to modify the hierarchy of ideal traits demanded most frequently. Explanation, organization, and knowledge of subject matter are of top importance to average and superior scholars, to men as well as women, to veterans and nonveterans, etc. At the other extreme, tolerance to disagreement and pleasing personality are the least frequently selected traits regardless of the student's status in any of these respects.

Attitudes toward instructional attributes in the social sciences are only slightly less consistent. The top three attributes (with minor variations in their rank order) are the same for all curricular groups, for all age and grade levels, for students with differing amounts of extracurricular activity, and for all class groups. Slight deviations from this pattern occur, however, in respect to sex and employment history. But in every segment of the student body studied, encouragement to thought and organization were included in the three traits most widely agreed upon as important. In a few instances, i.e., men, those having had full-time employment, and to some extent inferior scholars, explanations or knowledge of subject vied with or displaced tolerance to disagreement for inclusion in the top three. Furthermore, in virtually all student body segments, pleasing personality, fairness in tests, and attitude toward students were most infrequently cited as important.

Certain of the variables show more differences in student attitude toward instruction in arts courses, but again the over-all agreement is high. Among underclassmen, students inactive in extracurricular activities, and those of low scholarship, there is a slight tendency to place explanations above enthusiasm in the hierarchy of academic virtues. But in all segments of the student body, knowledge and encouragement to thought are most frequently voted among the top three attributes. Interestingly enough, only the highest scholarship group places encouragement to thought above knowledge of subject.

This over-all tendency toward consistency should not, however, be permitted to cover up certain illuminating differences in the frequency with which certain segments of the student body select or fail to select specific traits as being of high importance. Thus, for example, while superior and inferior scholars may both select encouragement to thought as one of the top three traits in an arts instructor, in fact a much higher proportion of the superior students named this trait and, on the other hand, a relatively large proportion of the inferior scholars felt that fairness in tests was of prime importance.

A few outstanding tendencies are also evidenced in the attitudes of various segments of the student body regardless of the type of course with which they are concerned. In the arts, sciences, and the social sciences, students of high scholastic standing named fairness as an important trait much less frequently than did poor scholars. Similarly, lowerclassmen named this same trait as important much more frequently than upperclassmen.

The only other student variable showing a consistent effect upon ideal instructional traits regardless of course type was that of age. Older students more frequently placed a high valuation upon organization of materials than did the younger.

While age and scholastic standing are the only variables affecting choice regardless of course area, several variables are associated with a common viewpoint in at least two course areas. For social sciences and arts, but not for physical sciences, low scholarship is

associated with a wider selection of explanations as an ideal instructional trait. Similarly, underclassmen more frequently than
juniors and seniors desire speaking ability in these areas. Upperclassmen, however, are more concerned with encouragement to
thinking and enthusiasm in both the social sciences and arts. For
instruction in these same two areas, men place more value upon
explanations while women more frequently cite enthusiasm as a
trait of high importance.

Significance of Student Expectations. Quite apart from these
constructs of good teaching, other and more generalized student
values may well be considered relevant to such an inquiry. Thus,
for example, two-thirds of the student body under investigation
were found to be motivated to seek a college education either for
specific vocational purposes or to obtain the necessary background for continuing their studies in a graduate or professional
school. And the majority would have come to college in preference
to "an interesting job at sixty-five dollars per week with a reasonable future."

The attitudes and opinions of such a serious minded and earnest
body of young people are important on almost any score. In a
day of endless confusion as to the proper ends and values of college education, their constructs of "good teaching" would seem
to have particular relevance. While it is clearly no part of the
thesis of this work that students have either the competence or
the ability to contribute to the resolution of this confusion, their
expectations, no matter how starry-eyed or immature, are part of
the materials from which the consensus will ultimately be woven.

7

WHAT THE STUDENT FINDS

IN view of the lack of general consensus in our society upon the goals of college instruction, it is not surprising that wide differences exist in students' minds as to the desirable characteristics of professors. Yet if agreement were to be deliberately sought on any single professional attribute, all interested groups—teachers, students, administrators, and the public—would probably concur upon that relatively tangible asset, knowledge of the subject matter or expertness in the field. No faculty, it is easily and obviously argued, is worth its salt if it doesn't know what it's talking about. But herein lies the rub. Knowledge is not necessarily enough for good teaching. The student who quipped, in speaking of one of his professors, "he sure knows his stuff but he's a lousy teacher," contributes eloquently to one aspect of our thesis.

It is the qualifying "but" that is of most interest. If a teacher has been able to convince his students that he knows his field adequately, but if, at the same time, his students remain unconvinced that he is able to explain it to them, what kind of a teacher is he? Or if a teacher is thought to be unfair, or intolerant, or impatient of students, or bored with his subject, or disorganized, the same disconcerting question presents itself. Teaching is a dynamic *gestalt*. It does not necessarily rest upon expertness alone.

The actual evaluations of the faculty under scrutiny were made on the ten different characteristics assumed to be of importance to good teaching. The objective, it should be remembered, was to provide a framework covering those aspects of instructional behavior both relevant to, and believed by the student to be relevant to, effective instruction.

The All-Faculty Position. The attribute upon which the faculty received highest evaluation by the students was knowledge of subject. The lowest score was upon ability to stimulate thinking. Thus, on a basis whereby a potential maximum score would be 100, the faculty averaged 88 on knowledge and 55 on stimulation to thinking. On no other traits was the faculty as a whole considered so outstanding as in subject matter competence, although a score of 78 was given on attitude toward the subject. On the other hand, students were almost as critical of their instructors in regard to their fairness on examinations as they were in respect to stimulation to thought.

Since instructional problems and purposes legitimately differ for the areas of instruction, it is essential that evaluations be considered separately for each of the broad academic fields. The overall evaluation, averaging the ratings on all attributes, is, however, very similar for the arts, sciences and the social sciences. Thus if all phases of instruction are considered, students indicate no significant difference in their estimation of the different areas of study. And, in fact, differences between areas on ratings for specific attributes are relatively unimportant.

Only for two of the qualities studied were there notable differences between the areas. In tolerance to disagreement social science instructors were rated somewhat higher than others, while in speaking ability they were lower. In each case the ratings of social science instructors deviated most markedly from the average of all.

The similarities, however, are much more striking than the differences in the three fields of study. Instruction in each area was most highly commended upon the same attribute, knowledge of subject, and likewise was most widely condemned upon a single attribute, stimulation to thought. Similarly the decided weakness on fairness in examinations is present in all areas, as is the relative strength in respect to attitude toward subject. The following table gives the *average* scores of the faculty on the ten attributes of teaching.

TABLE 5

AVERAGE SCORES OF THE FACULTY ON TEN ATTRIBUTES OF TEACHING

Knowledge of subject	88
Attitude toward subject	78
Organization of subject matter	75
Attitude toward students	72
Personality	72
Speaking ability	72
Ability to explain	71
Tolerance to disagreement	71
Fairness in examinations	60
Encouragement to thinking	55
Number of ratings	(6180) *

* This figure does not include teachers of education, and home economics courses.

Apart from the similarities in extreme scores, the most interesting comparisons lie in the relative standing of speaking ability and tolerance within the different areas. While arts instructors rated higher on "speaking ability" than in most other traits, this was one of the greater weaknesses in social science instruction. Tolerance to disagreement, however, was the third strongest asset of the social scientists and third greatest weakness of the arts instructors. It is interesting to note that as attractive personalities, arts instructors are less favorably noted than others, especially science teachers. (See pp. 63–65 for median scores of arts, science, and social science professors.)

In spite of these outstanding differences in ranking of qualities, it is apparent that students have much the same criticisms and commendations to offer their instructors regardless of the instructional field. The relative pattern of consistency in the responses is the most striking, yet at the same time the most disconcerting, aspect of the findings.

TABLE 6

SCORES OF ARTS, SCIENCE, AND SOCIAL TEACHERS ON THREE
ATTRIBUTES OF TEACHING

	Arts Teachers	*Science Teachers*	*Soc. Sci. Teachers*
Speaking ability	75	73	68
Tolerance to disagreement	68	70	76
Personality	70	76	73
Number of ratings	(2685)	(1568)	(1927)

Factors Associated with the Ratings. The evaluations given teachers are not to be taken as objective truths; they are undoubtedly subject to individual student bias as well as to external conditions affecting the teacher-student relationship. Although it would be manifestly impossible to enter into a study of all possible factors conditioning the student's evaluation, certain of the most reasonable influencing conditions can be analyzed in terms of the data at hand. In that context we have considered specifically the effect of the student's scholastic standing in the course, sex, year in college, the size of the class, and whether or not it was a required course. Class size is of course an external limiting condition upon the teacher's opportunity to manifest certain qualities, while the other factors might well reflect student bias in evaluation. As we shall see, the student's grade standing in the course was by far the most important conditioner of his ratings.

On every teaching attribute evaluated, save one, students with low scholastic standing in the course were more critical in their judgments than the better scholars. Only in ratings of knowledge of subject did all scholarship groups agree on the level of their instructors' competence. This condition is true for each area of instruction. There is, in other words, no indication that a grade bias was more pronounced for one field of study than for another. On the other hand, this bias was considerably more evident in the ratings on certain attributes than in others.

As one might expect, the greatest range in evaluation is to be found in fairness on examinations. Here the bias exerted by the student's grade position is at least twice as great as that in most other attributes. In evaluations of the teacher's attitude toward the student, which is undoubtedly closely related in student eyes to examination marks, differences are likewise quite large in each area of instruction.

TABLE 7

SCORES GIVEN INSTRUCTORS IN TWO ATTRIBUTES OF TEACHING BY STUDENTS OF VARIOUS SCHOLASTIC STANDINGS *

	Fairness in Examinations	Attitude toward Students	Number of Ratings †
Scores given			
Arts Teachers by:			
Superior students	65	74	(1258)
Average students	59	72	(713)
Poor students	53	65	(502)
Science Teachers			
Superior students	66	79	(736)
Average students	57	73	(360)
Poor students	54	69	(390)
Social Sci. Teachers			
Superior students	68	77	(806)
Average students	62	70	(549)
Poor students	55	68	(407)

* Students receiving an average grade of "B" or better are designated "superior," those receiving "B—" or "C+" are called "average," while "poor" refers to all students whose average grade is "C" or less.
† 459 students failed to estimate scholastic standing in course.

In general, while the influence of grades upon evaluations is clear, it is not of great magnitude. Thus in most evaluations the lowest grade group evaluated the instructor only five or six points lower than did the highest grade scholars. While a grade bias exists, low grades apparently have not equally influenced student estimates in the various items.

Thus if we turn to evaluations of speaking ability, knowledge of subject, and attitude toward subject, areas not directly associated with students' classroom standing, we find the maximum deviation between high and low scholars to be six points, and in most instances it is much less.

TABLE 8

SCORES GIVEN INSTRUCTORS IN THREE ATTRIBUTES OF TEACHING BY STUDENTS OF VARIOUS SCHOLASTIC STANDINGS

	Speaking Ability	Knowledge of Subject	Attitude Twd. Subj.	Number of Ratings
Scores given Arts Teachers by:				
Superior students	74	89	81	(1258)
Average students	74	87	77	(713)
Poor students	72	89	76	(502)
Science Teachers:				
Superior students	76	88	79	(736)
Average students	73	88	76	(360)
Poor students	69	89	76	(390)
Social Sci. Teachers:				
Superior students	70	88	81	(806)
Average students	68	88	79	(549)
Poor students	66	89	77	(407)

It is quite reasonable to suppose that a low grade student would, quite honestly, and in his own eyes objectively, find his instructor deficient in explanatory ability, fairness, and attitude toward the student. Fully as significant as the grade bias here is the fact that such a bias was no greater than it appears to be.

Further it should be noted that although the low grade students were more critical, they differed slightly from superior scholars in their judgments of relative strength and weakness in their instructors. Thus both the highest and lowest grade groups gave their lowest evaluations, in each area, upon stimulus to thinking, and their highest upon knowledge of subject. Similarly high grade students, as well as low grade, judged fairness in examinations to be their instructors' next most serious weakness.

While in general the effect of class standing upon evaluation is very similar regardless of the area of instruction, some notable differences between areas exist. Thus the grades held by students appear to influence evaluations of explanatory ability in social science instructors somewhat less than in other areas. On the other hand, all grade levels tend to rate science instructors high in their personality attraction. And there is practically no difference between grade levels in their tendency to give high ratings to arts instructors on speaking ability. These are, however, isolated exceptions to the general similarity for different areas in effects of scholarship upon evaluations. These results, consequently, throw some light on one of the perennial problems of the teacher: what to do about, and how to reach better, the poorer students. Insofar as the data suggest generalizable clews, special efforts on the part of the professor to convince his weaker students that he is a man of great learning and that he has a sound attitude toward his subject, will avail him little. Nor is "improved" speaking ability likely to raise his status in the students' eyes. On the other hand, these materials suggest that much might be gained by giving special attention to a better understanding of his grading and examination "folkways," and that a genuinely sympathetic attitude toward such students, while costing nothing, may pay high dividends. That neither of these efforts on the part of the professor will turn poor students into superior ones is almost too obvious to mention. But insofar as poor students are "poor" because of barriers and resistances in the teacher-student relationship, such efforts may be very much to the point.

Finally, however, it should be pointed out again that these apparent grade biases are neither great nor completely consistent. While most other studies (see Chapter 3) have tended to disavow their existence, those reported here do seem to have both logical meaning and some significance to a better understanding of teacher-student relationships.

Another perplexing and recurrent professional problem is the question of optimum class size. Although student evaluations could not be interpreted as offering any definitive answers to this question, they might, perhaps, be thought to have some relevance.

In this connection, however, differences in evaluation depending upon size of class are surprisingly slight. Nor is there justification for assuming that the small class (under twenty) leads to more or less favorable impressions of the teacher. Differences, where they occur, are usually erratic.

Students in classes under twenty rate their arts instructors quite high, interestingly enough, in speaking ability, but for other attributes the differences are unimportant. In science courses students tend to find the best organization of materials and greatest knowledge of subject in large classes. But they also find large classes associated with less fairness in examinations and less encouragement to thinking. Class size has little to do with evaluations in the social sciences except that students in the small classes rate their instructors relatively high in their encouragement to thought. It should be noted, however, that, although they find more encouragement to thinking in the small classes, ratings are still lower than on the other attributes.

With these few exceptions—and most of them seem reasonable and understandable—size of class appears to have little to do with student estimates. Students, apparently, know quite well whom they consider to be the good teachers regardless of how many fellow students there may be in any particular class.

Still a different kind of professorial concern centers around a frequently heard contention that students who are "required" to take certain courses not only are harder to teach but may even be subconsciously resentful of their teachers.

It might, thus, be hypothecated that courses taken as electives (in contrast to required) would be more highly evaluated since they are the result of student choice among alternatives. The discovered differences between the two types of classes, however, are generally small and inconclusive. Among social science instructors, for example, there is some slight evidence that ratings tend to be higher by students taking the courses as electives, whereas science ratings tend to be slightly higher among those taking the courses as required. But in both of these cases the differences are small and erratic and forbid any conclusive statement.

It is also clear that neither sex nor class in college influences the ratings which students assign their instructors. While some differences appear between the ratings of the various classes, these are small and erratic fluctuations. There is no evidence that either sex or advancement in college program influences judgments of instructors. This stands, it is to be recalled, in some contrast to the differences between such groups in their ideal constructs of college teachers.

Significance of the Ratings. Perhaps no greater student tribute could be paid to a faculty than to have it held in high esteem on the issue of subject matter competence. Certainly in the present study, the student body has little complaint on this score. Throughout all areas of instruction faculty members, on the average, were universally scored high on a scale indicative of competence in their respective fields. Yet sheer subject matter expertness, as we have earlier suggested, is not necessarily enough for good teaching.

While these ratings, of course, take on their greatest significance as providing new insights for the individual teacher, their composite importance theoretically should lie in comparative differences. But it is on this point that the findings are both surprising and interesting. They are remarkable in their homogeneity. Although social science teachers were judged, relatively speaking, to be more tolerant to disagreement, and arts teachers to be more effective in speaking ability, the differences among the three major fields of instruction were, on the whole, slight. This very pattern of consistency lends weight to the results insofar as one is tempted to generalize from them. Since the students were known, through various tests applied to the detailed ratings, to make effective discrimination in their judgments, the similarity in the average scores from field to field is striking. It represents a further, though indirect, corroboration of the meaningfulness of the various dimensions of teaching selected for study. Not that these dimensions necessarily constitute *the* criteria of good teaching, rather that they make sense, in students' minds, as significant and important attributes.

Finally, in any over-all sense, the relationship between what the student finds in his teacher and what he expects, is the most pertinent clew to the student's estimate of the whole process. This comparison of the discovered with the expected is the subject of the next chapter.

8

The Ideal vs. the Actual

IF student opinion has been neglected in connection with the problem of the quality of college teaching, the neglect has harmed the teacher as much as the student. The traffic of teaching does not travel a one way street. Students are not, in reality, as one teacher recently remarked, "like potted plants waiting to be sprinkled with knowledge." Education is a process involving more than the giving out and soaking up of information. It necessitates an interaction of human beings and neither party to the relationship can be thought of in sterile or inanimate terms. In short, what the student thinks of his teacher is important. His case for a fair hearing on this count is clear.

The utility to individual instructors of student opinion at this level, in providing new insights and understandings of the teaching problem, will be discussed below in some detail. Yet obviously no mere collection of student ratings of instructors has any claim to importance or validity as an overall measure of teaching quality. The more general aspect of the student's point of view in terms of what he thinks he wants from his teacher is of equal significance. The dream must be balanced against the reality. The one attitude complements the other. The student's construct of ideal teaching can only have its true value in relation to what he thinks he is getting in fact.

The actual scores therefore take on their greatest meaning when studied in reference to standards by which the various attributes may themselves be evaluated. Thus it is not to be supposed that fairness on examinations is to be equated with knowledge of subject in any evaluation of effective teaching. While it is quite conceivable that fairly wide consensus upon the relative significance of these attributes for the various fields might be found among educators, the standards imposed by the students themselves are considerably more relevant in the present context. In the comparison of the student's ideal construct of the instructor with his concrete evaluations, we can lay bare a wide area of potential tensions, dissatisfactions, and ineffectiveness in the teacher-student relationship. This implies neither that the student evaluation of the teacher is objectively accurate nor that the student's ideal construct conforms to more mature judgments. These issues are simply irrelevant in an inquiry of this kind.

In an earlier chapter we have noted the attributes which students believe are most significant for instructors in the various areas of study. Table 9 shows the rank order of importance of the various attributes, together with the rank order of actual scores of instructors on these same attributes. While this method of presentation allows only a rough comparison, it serves our purposes in emphasizing both the divergencies and similarities between what the student wants and what he thinks he is getting. Thus for both the arts and sciences, two of the top three ideal characteristics are found to be similarly rated in actuality, whereas for the social sciences only one of the ideal attributes is among the three given highest ratings in the actual scores.

Perfect conformity in the rank order of preference and the order of actual ratings probably could not reasonably be expected. But some of the differences (the capitalized items) are so striking as to suggest serious inconsistencies. Generally speaking, there seems a closer conformity between the desired attributes and the discovered ones among arts than among science or social science instructors.

These relationships suggest the following observations which, though not statistically conclusive, summarize current student reaction to the specific faculty under consideration:

1. Students want a high level of scholarly competence in their instructors and, according to their own testimony, they are finding it. In fact, relative to some other qualities thought to be important, the faculty may even be thought to exceed student expectation in this regard.

2. Students place high value upon that type of teaching which stimulates individual thought, and it is on this score that the faculty fails most strikingly to meet student demand. This discrepancy is particularly serious in the social sciences and arts.

3. Students also want teachers who have the ability to offer adequate explanations of their subject matter, and with the exception of science teachers, the faculty approximates student expectations. In the science field, however, the discrepancy is wide and possibly serious.

4. Students attach importance to the ability of a teacher to organize his materials, and generally speaking, the faculty position in this respect matches the intensity of student desires.

5. Students place some value upon the enthusiasm of a teacher for his subject, and, relative to other criteria, the faculty comes up to these expectations—particularly in the social sciences.

6. Students feel that sympathetic professional attitudes and personal attractiveness are relatively unimportant to good teaching, yet, on the whole, the faculty was rated considerably higher in these attributes than in certain traits the students felt to be more basic.

7. Although students feel that fairness in examinations is not necessarily an important attribute of good teaching, it is per-

haps of more than passing interest that the faculty was consistently rated low on this score.

TABLE 9

RANK ORDER OF IDEAL AND ACTUAL TRAITS

Arts Teachers

Ideal	Actual
Knowledge of subject	Knowledge of subject
ENCOURAGEMENT TO THOUGHT	Attitude toward subject
Attitude toward subject	Speaking ability
Ability to explain	Organization
Organization	Ability to explain
Speaking ability	Attitude toward students
Personality	Personality
Tolerance to disagreement	Tolerance to disagreement
Attitude toward students	Fairness in examinations
Fairness in examinations	ENCOURAGEMENT TO THOUGHT

Science Teachers

Ideal	Actual
ABILITY TO EXPLAIN	Knowledge of subject
Organization	Organization
Knowledge of subject	Attitude toward subject
Encouragement to thought	Personality
Attitude toward subject	Attitude toward students
Fairness in examinations	Speaking ability
Speaking ability	Tolerance to disagreement
Attitude toward students	ABILITY TO EXPLAIN
Personality	Fairness in examinations
Tolerance to disagreement	Encouragement to thought

Social Science Teachers

Ideal	Actual
ENCOURAGEMENT TO THOUGHT	Knowledge of subject
Organization	Attitude toward subject
Tolerance to disagreement	Tolerance to disagreement
Knowledge of subject	Organization
Ability to explain	Personality
Attitude toward subject	Attitude toward students
Speaking ability	Ability to explain
Fairness in examinations	Speaking ability
Personality	Fairness in examinations
Attitude toward students	ENCOURAGEMENT TO THOUGHT

Such observations as the above, of course, have no claim to validity other than to the particular student body and faculty under study. They do, however, suggest some hypotheses which, if they were to receive validation on the basis of future studies, would constitute shattering indictments of the American system of higher education. Clearly the most important of these has to do with that teaching attribute referred to here as the ability to encourage thought.

The twentieth century reaction against an educational theory which emphasized "mental" discipline, the training of the intellectual faculties, and even moral habits, places a new type of responsibility upon the contemporary teacher. His job is "not to impose tasks for which the student sees no value but to create an environment and determine surroundings that will help him build a coherent and interested self. . . ." [1] Today such an aim, in spite of the bitter controversies centering on educational goals and instructional "systems," receives widespread acceptance. Society does not want the kind of person who has been compelled, through fear of ridicule or punishment, to think along lines set by an arbitrary authority. Rather its educational institutions are designed to stimulate the ability to make intelligent decisions and choices. In this connection, perhaps one of the basic weaknesses in traditional educational theory was that it failed to consider the potentials and purposes of students. It assumed the desirability of certain types of pedagogical practices regardless of how students might be affected. Subject matters were considered ends in themselves and, regardless of the capacities, interests, and needs of individual students, the "stuff" of knowledge was handed out to be learned.

To this position, Dewey has a penetrating reply,

There is, I think, no point in the philosophy of progressive education which is sounder than its emphasis upon the importance of the participation of the learner in the formation of purposes which direct his learning, . . . just as there is no defect in traditional education greater than its failure to secure the active cooperation of the pupil in construction of the purposes involved in his studying.[2]

What Dewey is saying has as much to do with teaching as with learning. While his emphasis is upon a new recognition of freedom for the student, he is in no sense advocating the license of self-orientation which perhaps legitimately has been charged to the earlier progressives. The teacher has more than a trivial role to play. Guidance and planning are necessary components. No orderly expansion and development of a subject matter is otherwise possible, and certainly not one within which the student is capable of thinking for himself.

Even though such a resolution of this aspect of educational theory be found unacceptable by some contemporary teachers, the data from the present survey unmistakably point to its widespread acceptance among students. From teachers of social sciences, this ability to encourage individual thinking is the one quality most widely wanted. From teachers of the humanities and arts it ranks second only to subject matter competence. And even from science teachers, where the subject matter is popularly regarded as more exact and fixed, it is a teaching trait highly regarded. Yet it is on this very dimension of teaching that the faculties of each of these subject matter fields received the least amount of student applause.

If this result is to be viewed as a symptomatic clew to an understanding of higher education in general, the situation is indeed serious. In such terms, students become "marginal" people. They are caught between two conflicting cultural pressures. They face daily the inconsistency between means and ends.

Regardless of which side is "right," such a situation has reality and calls for resolution. Though an ideological resolution may be slow in coming, since it obviously involves basic educational concepts, some practical compromises in the immediate future are indicated. It is now a matter of common knowledge that any kind of emotional or nervous tension produces changes in intellectual activities and abilities. Thus if students, in fact, are found to be disturbed by this pattern of inconsistency between experience and expectation, the basic welfare of higher education is at stake. Not only do the levels of intellectual attainment stand to suffer, but the very goals of education are placed in jeopardy.

A similar, though perhaps somewhat less serious, inconsistency between the actual and the ideal from the student point of view has to do with the ability of science teachers to offer adequate explanations. Rated as the most important attribute in the hierarchy of desired qualities, it ranks among the lowest in terms of the actual scores.

The potential significance of this discrepancy is not readily apparent except in terms of the trite observation that we live in a scientific world—a world whose values and activities are basically oriented to science. Although such an environment offers a kind of security by virtue of the exactness of the principles to which it is geared, it is in reality characterized by constant flux. New developments and discoveries produce anything but a static world. To all of this the average individual must make an adjustment. Nor is the college student excepted. He faces the same problems, only more so. Yet presumably he is among those whose educational opportunities are such as to give a comparative advantage for living in a complex society.

If, consequently, he feels an instructional inadequacy with respect to his chances for gaining an *understanding* of science—if he feels that his teachers are lacking in some basic ability to explain—then again the educational system is within the focus of a potentially critical spotlight. Science is said to dispel superstition and ignorance, but insofar as the students of science themselves feel the handicap of complexity and are psychologically ready to take its postulates and findings for granted in lieu of satisfactory explanations, it may well become a breeder of superstition and non-logical thought.

The accuracy or inaccuracy of such a charge is irrelevant to the discussion. It is how the student reacts that counts. He may be dead wrong but that does not by one iota change the process by which he is presumably becoming an "educated" person. Whatever may be the ultimate and objective consensus as to what constitutes good teaching, it is certain that students' ideas and reactions will always be closely correlated to the effectiveness with which the teaching is done.

9

WHO ARE THE GOOD TEACHERS?

IF great teachers are rare, what rewards lie hidden for the rank and file? The profession calls many, and for the sincere teacher no nobler task exists than that of helping to pass on the heritage of learning. But the task becomes increasingly difficult and the professorial way of life less well defined. The job may be noble, yet this very consideration increases its hazards. Both the confusions of a rapidly changing society and the uncertainties of educational goals add to potential discouragement. Yet the assumption of this volume is basically optimistic. Our thesis is simple and essentially obvious. We believe that the good teacher is self-created, that his rewards are infinitely great and that more insight into the currently neglected side of the teaching process will go far toward telling teachers how to attain these rewards.

The professorial image as seen through students' eyes is rarely clear-cut. A teacher's evaluation is not typically a phenomenon of unanimity of response. He is well liked for some things and disliked for others. His rating depends sometimes upon the classroom situation, sometimes upon the nature of the course he is teaching, sometimes upon the quality of his students. But none of these relationships are definitive. Another variable is the instructor himself.

What, if any, are the faculty characteristics commonly associated with good student evaluations? Specifically, is there any relationship between the quality of teaching (as estimated by students) and such professorial characteristics as age, experience, academic rank, college degrees, and publications? In the students' eyes who are the good teachers? Findings of the Brooklyn project give some indication:

Age. That a relationship exists between an instructor's age and his reported effectiveness as a teacher is brought into sharp relief in this study when the faculty ratings of older, middle-aged, and young instructors are compared. Table 10 shows the percentage of faculty members in the three age groups who were rated above the median for their major field in each of the ten attributes studied.

TABLE 10

FACULTY RATINGS ACCORDING TO AGE OF INSTRUCTORS †

	20–39	40–49	50–69
Percent above median in: *			
Organization	60%	49%	38%
Speaking ability	56	54	37
Ability to explain	58	50	39
Encouragement to thinking	50	54	45
Attitude toward students	54	48	45
Knowledge of subject	38	63	57
Attitude toward subject	54	48	45
Fairness in examinations	51	50	42
Tolerance to disagreement	59	50	34
Personality	57	49	36
100% =	(162)	(144)	(78)

† Data on age not available for 7 faculty members.
* In this table and those that follow the medians were computed separately for each of the three fields of instruction. Thus each faculty member for the purposes of these comparisons is above or below the median for his field.

With but one exception, younger instructors are rated superior teachers. That exception, however, is a notable one, for it is in knowledge of the subject that older men excel. But, even here, the 40–49 age group claims a slightly greater proportion above the median than does the group 50–69. It is quite clear, then, that even if, in the eyes of the student, the older teacher knows more, he is regarded as less successful on other counts.

Moreover, far from being confined to such teaching attributes as tolerance to disagreement and personality, where one might normally expect the youthful instructor to show an advantage, the young teacher holds just as great an advantage over his older colleagues in such qualities as organization of subject matter, ability to explain, and speaking ability. Less striking but nevertheless significant are his generally more sympathetic attitude toward his students, his greater enthusiasm for his subject, and his fairness in examinations.

This trend is not, of course, necessarily a result of age as such; it does not necessarily mean that a man becomes a less effective teacher as he grows older. It may well result from some more basic tendency, such as the improving standards of teacher training, or the more stringent selective process by which the younger teachers were chosen.

Rank. Among the various descriptive data available for each instructor, perhaps the most basic criterion of his ability and experience is his academic rank. Although in specific instances the validity of such a measure is obviously open to question, when applied to a group of some four hundred individuals the classification is undoubtedly meaningful.

If any one fact stands out, it is that students' estimates of scholarship are clearly reflected in actual academic rank. Eighty-five per cent of the full professors are rated above the median in knowledge of the subject. Only half of the instructors and one-fifth of those below instructor level placed above the median. Between these extremes, associate and assistant professors carried out the positive relationship between academic rank and student evaluation of scholarship.

On the other hand, the same tendency that was noted with respect to age (with which rank is, of course, intercorrelated) is repeated in the breakdown of instructors by academic rank. In

TABLE 11

PROPORTION OF INSTRUCTORS OF VARIOUS ACADEMIC RANKS RATED
ABOVE MEDIAN IN KNOWLEDGE OF SUBJECT

		N *
Professor	85%	(20)
Associate professor	64	(25)
Assistant professor	62	(125)
Instructor	51	(131)
Other Ranks	21	(90)

* Tables 12, 13, and 14 are based on the same N's.

every case, except knowledge of the subject, higher rank tends either to be associated with lower ratings or to have no consistent relationship with student definitions of good teaching.

Notwithstanding the student recognition of superior knowledge on the part of faculty members of higher standing, only slightly more than a third of the full professors were rated above average in their enthusiasm toward the subject they teach; about half of those below the rank of associate professor were judged above average.

TABLE 12

PROPORTION OF INSTRUCTORS OF VARIOUS ACADEMIC RANKS RATED
ABOVE MEDIAN IN ATTITUDE TOWARD SUBJECT

Professor	35%
Associate professor	44
Assistant professor	52
Instructor	49
Other ranks	55

The student, as well as the subject, is also apparently of less concern to college teachers of higher rank: only a third of the professors but almost as many as three out of every five instructors were considered above average in their sympathetic approach to the individual student. (Table 13.) Similarly, but not surprising in view of the other findings, a negative relationship was found between academic rank and student ratings of a teacher's personality. (Table 14.)

Tolerance to disagreement appears to be most frequently regarded as a quality of the teacher of lower rank and, interestingly enough, while all other teachers were very equally distributed

TABLE 13

PROPORTION OF INSTRUCTORS OF VARIOUS ACADEMIC RANKS RATED
ABOVE MEDIAN IN ATTITUDE TOWARD STUDENTS

Professor	35%
Associate professor	44
Assistant professor	44
Instructor	56
Other ranks	54

above and below the median in ability to explain, only 40 per cent of the full professors were judged better than the median score.

TABLE 14

PROPORTION OF INSTRUCTORS OF VARIOUS ACADEMIC RANKS RATED
ABOVE MEDIAN IN PERSONALITY

Professor	35%
Associate professor	44
Assistant professor	50
Instructor	48
Other ranks	56

Since there is a close correlation between academic rank and age, and since a close similarity was found between the two breakdowns, age was held constant, as shown in Table 15, within each step of the progression from instructor to full professor. Although the numbers of full professors and of associates were too small to allow for further statistical refinement by age, the two lower ranks were investigated. On that basis, there seems to be no evidence to doubt that rank has a meaning of its own, independent of age. Thus, young assistant professors are rated higher in knowledge of the subject than are young instructors; middle-aged assistant professors surpass middle-aged instructors; and older assistant professors outstrip older instructors two to one.

Where the differences based on rank were significant, the elimination of the influence of age did not, save for a few specific deviations, alter the relationship between assistant professors and instructors. Thus subject matter competence appears to have played a very real role in the process of academic promotion. The implication, however, is strong that other relevant characteristics of the

TABLE 15

PROPORTION OF INSTRUCTORS AND ASSISTANT PROFESSORS OF
VARIOUS AGES RATED ABOVE MEDIAN IN KNOWLEDGE

		N*
20–39 years		
Assistant professor	61%	(28)
Instructor	54	(55)
40–49 years		
Assistant professor	65	(70)
Instructor	56	(53)
50–69 years		
Assistant professor	60	(25)
Instructor	32	(19)

* Data on age not available for 6 faculty members.

good teacher, at least from the student point of view, have, at the same time, perhaps been disregarded.

Academic degrees. Although somewhat related to academic rank, the formal academic degrees of the faculty were also balanced against student ratings. In some respects the relationships based on age and academic rank are repeated; in other respects, formal academic attainment appears to be a more consistent factor in student estimates of teaching ability than either of the other two.

With the exception of a less sympathetic attitude toward one's students, the possession of a doctorate is apparently something more than a symbol. The data give evidence that there are real values attached to the Ph.D. in terms of better scholarship and the ability to transmit it, for the Ph.D.'s surpassed all others in nine out of the ten qualities of good teaching.

Curiously, however, the Ph.D.'s were followed, and occasionally very closely followed, not by those holding master's degrees, but by the youngest and perhaps least experienced members of the faculty, the bachelors. A possible explanation of this phenomenon may lie in the fact that the possessors of the baccalaureate alone are very young and promising persons belonging to a small and highly selected group.

Differences based on students' evaluation of the instructor's level of information are even more conspicuous than in other comparisons. More than two out of every three Ph.D.'s, but only about one master or bachelor out of every four was judged above average in knowledge of the subject. Although the instructor with a doctorate degree held his advantage in nearly all other areas of instruction, his superiority was never so pronounced.

TABLE 16

PROPORTION OF INSTRUCTORS HOLDING VARIOUS ACADEMIC DEGREES
WHO WERE RATED ABOVE MEDIAN IN KNOWLEDGE OF SUBJECT

		N *
Bachelor's degree	25%	(40)
Master's	27	(122)
Doctorate	68	(210)

* Excluding 19 faculty members for whom data were not available.

Of the ten criteria, knowledge of the subject is perhaps the most clearly defined and clearly understood. The results indicate that it is also the most stable. But of greater significance is the suggestion that faculty characteristics commonly associated with *general* teaching ability and experience are in fact very *specific* measures of scholarship. To be sure, the more experienced teacher is the better informed, and the data leave no doubt of student recognition of this fact. From the student point of view, however, scholarship is not enough. And, clearly, many of the criteria of good teaching are not the product of experience; on the contrary, the further away the instructor moves from the student in terms of age and information and experience, the more difficult it appears to be for him to understand the needs of his students. This is not to minimize the importance of knowledge of the subject, but to emphasize that the recognized *scholar* is not always thought to be the most able *teacher*.

Finally, as in the analysis of academic rank, age was held constant within each academic degree, in order to make certain that the above-noted differences were not merely reflections of age.

Again, the data indicate that on the whole the differences based on college degree are real. In all age groups, the relationships between Ph.D.'s and masters remain essentially the same as those observed between Ph.D.'s and masters as a whole. And although in organization of subject matter and in ability to explain, young M.A.'s surpass young B.A.'s, still, in the great majority of instances, the apparently highly selected bachelors hold their superiority over the masters.

Published Research. Research ability was another characteristic of both interest and concern which was examined with some care. With the increasing confusion as to the "conflict" between teaching and research, it is of more than passing interest to know whether teachers who do research and are successful in publishing the results are any more successful *qua* teachers in the students' eyes than their nonresearching colleagues. While, to be sure, this characteristic is probably closely related to some of the factors discussed above, it seems worth investigation.

Research ability, as measured (crudely by the presence or absence of published works) does seem to be at least partially related to students' ratings. The following table shows this relationship for three items. Only on one teaching attribute, namely attitude toward students, does the relationship go the other way.

TABLE 17

FACULTY RATINGS ON THREE ITEMS
BY AGE AND PUBLICATIONS *

	20–39		40–49		50–69	
	Publications	No Publ.	Publications	No Publ.	Publications	No Publ.
Per cent above median in:						
Organization	70%	56%	62%	38%	49%	31%
Ability to explain	70	55	57	43	43	36
Knowledge of subject	67	30	75	52	66	50
100% =	(33)	(129)	(68)	(75)	(35)	(42)

* Data on age and publications not available for 9 faculty members.

In short, research ability (as thus measured) appears to have a real bearing upon the students' conception of the good teacher. Like the Ph.D., research activity on the part of the teacher seems to have more than a symbolic value.

Good Teachers and Great Teachers. Despite the relationships between these few faculty characteristics and student ratings, as described above, the foregoing discussion strongly urges the conclusion that the great teacher is not to be recognized in terms of any one set of objective criteria. He may, in fact, be young or old, active or inactive in research, a Ph.D. or simply an A.B. Other than such obviously measurable traits are at work in producing the great teacher. Whatever may be one's theory of genius, these statistics, though pointing to some over-all trends, suggest agreement with President Butler's comment,

Of great teachers there are not very many in a generation, and nothing is more certain than that such are born and not made. Of good teachers there are, on the other hand, a fair supply. These are the men and women who, by reason of sound if somewhat partial knowledge, orderly-mindedness, skill in simple and clear presentation, and a gift of sympathy, are able to stimulate youth to study and to think.[1]

The implication is clear that while "great" teachers are born, "good" teachers are made. To most, at least, this should be a cheering hypothesis. In any event, it is the contention of this volume.

The academic labor going into the winning of a higher degree or the bringing to completion of a piece of research is apparently not without its rewards in the classroom. Thus the teacher who finds a place for himself in the wider world of scholarship will discover that he fares better with his students. This, it is reasonable to assume, he can do something about. He may never have been destined to play the role of a great teacher, but through various means and insights he can become far better than adequate.

The story of how one faculty reacted to a series of student ratings in their various interrelationships is the subject for the next chapter.

The one disconcerting finding, however, which protrudes from these statistics with compelling consistency relates to professorial age. Older teachers, these particular figures tell us, are thought to be more competent subject-wise, but in other respects they tend to be judged harshly. Perhaps President Butler anticipated this result when he spoke of "partial knowledge" as frequently characterizing the successful teacher. But irrespective of how competent a teacher must be in his own field, the question of age remains unanswered. Is it a dilemma of wisdom versus vitality? Is it a reflection of a secular trend in American culture toward a high evaluation on youth? Or is it a finding restricted to this particular faculty?

Youth will be served, we are told, but until further data are brought to bear on this point, older teachers have cause to be doubly aware of what their students think.

10

TEACHER REACTIONS TO STUDENT RATINGS

WHILE the findings reported in Part III are, in a sense, the distillation of student opinion and have many interesting potentialities as a general administrative guide for the improvement of instruction, they are, nevertheless, a by-product. The main objective, the *raison d'être,* of the investigation was the individual instructor and his self-improvement. The project aimed at the betterment of teacher-student relationships through a broader appreciation of the teacher's effect on his audience.

With the individual instructor in proper focus, at the center of the stage, it becomes apparent that any real validation of an inquiry of this kind must come from him. To the extent that he is stimulated to improve his teaching techniques, such a project may be called a success. If, however, it were possible to repeat such studies, a comparison of the results at two different points of time would perhaps constitute the strongest proof of validity and utility.

And interestingly enough, one member of the faculty under study was in a position to throw some light upon the temporal aspects of such a project. In commenting upon his ratings, he reports:

Ten years ago, while a member of the faculty of —————— University, a similar study, though on a miniature scale in comparison, was conducted. I have been fascinated by your report to me of student reaction to my teaching, because it would seem that I benefited greatly from student criticism that re-directed my emphases.

In lieu of such evidence on any systematic scale, however, some tangible demonstration of the effectiveness of the project may very well come from the immediate reactions of the instructors themselves. Thus some six months after he received his confidential rating, a personal letter was sent to each instructor asking for comments on the project and how, if at all, the data had been utilized. More specifically, the letter asked the following questions:

1. In general, do you feel that similar surveys in other institutions would be valuable?
2. Would you personally find it useful to have another set of student ratings sometime in the future?
3. In what ways, if any, have these materials or ratings been useful to you or given you added insights into the problems of teaching?

The excellent response (about three-fourths replied) attests to the widespread interest in the project on the part of the faculty. Furthermore there was no apparent bias in the return. Recipients of both low and high ratings replied in approximately proper proportion. But even more gratifying was the tenor of the replies: two out of every three voted in favor of *both* repeating the survey at Brooklyn College and conducting a similar one in another institution. Only 15 per cent were opposed to both proposals.[1] But the figures tell only a small part of the story. The individual instructor states his case eloquently, for no matter what his point of view—whether he feels the ratings were a waste of time and the money better spent on "books for the library," or whether he is convinced that his students' opinions have pointed the way to a more effective and satisfying teaching career—he is not disinterested. He may not yet have come to any specific conclusion about the utility of student evaluations, he may have some reservations about the particular form of the questionnaire used, or he may even question the validity of the results, but whatever his stand, he is intensely concerned. Teaching is an important part of his life; he is anxious to speak his mind.

The Minority Opposition. While surprisingly few instructors took the attitude that "students have nothing to teach me," a variation on that theme was the idea that teachers are well aware of their own strengths and weaknesses without going through the motions of a student opinion survey. Some were relieved to have their self-evaluations confirmed; others, more confident, found such reassurance unnecessary. An experienced English instructor states his position clearly:

For many years I have been aware of both my abilities and my shortcomings as a teacher. As a student and as a teacher in college, I early obtained many clear insights into the problems of teaching! During my twenty-five years as a college teacher of English, I have given about an equal amount of attention to subject-matter and method.

According to an assistant professor of history, held in high esteem by his students, the reports were useless both to instructors who know their abilities and to those who don't:

The ratings do not reveal information to the instructor that he doesn't already know unless the instructor is capable of self-delusion, and in that case he rationalizes the unpleasant findings.

In great detail a teacher of chemistry explains why student ratings cannot contribute to his instructional improvement:

I do not believe that a second set of ratings would be of great value to me. I have seen this chemistry work presented by a great many teachers, many of them of high national standing, and literally by dozens of new teachers whom I have had to observe in the last ten years. I have tried all the standard variations of presentation and checked the results against student response. I have checked content against the American Chemical Society standardized tests and against content in many of the larger universities and texts, and against needs in the advanced courses. Our examinations have been gone over by the Brooklyn College Office on Examinations in great detail. . . . I have, of course, been interested in seeing student reaction to all these things as well as to all the other methods we have been using as shown by your survey. I feel, by now, that I am a far better judge than the student of what he should have presented to him, how it should be presented, and how he should be examined on it. There is little opportunity for factual disagreement in the work which I am teaching. . . . I do not believe that a future check would vary enough in my case to make it worthwhile. . . .

Interestingly enough, the chemistry professor's students are in substantial agreement with him on most items, although, with surprising shrewdness, they recommended greater tolerance to disagreement and a generally more sympathetic attitude toward students.

A more concise though no less resolute refusal to concede to student opinion was made by a psychology instructor who suffered seriously at the hands of his raters. Judged very competent in organization of subject matter, on no other attribute did the instructor rise above the halfway mark for his field. Eight out of ten ratings, in fact, were in the lowest quartile. "The ratings," he declared, "confirmed what I already knew, but have no desire to change."

The over-all question of the validity of student ratings was raised by a number of the faculty. Taken together with specific criticisms of the questionnaire and other methodological techniques, these two problems almost completely cover the stated reasons behind unfavorable reactions to the survey. Even among the favorably inclined faculty members, qualifications or reservations are occasionally made in terms of methodology techniques or student competence to judge teaching ability. The former category of criticisms contained many helpful suggestions for improving and extending the research methods. They will be discussed further in the last chapter.

The question of student competence to pass judgment on teaching ability evoked several colorful responses. A professor of natural science, for example, complains with feeling:

A good teacher, according to students, is one who does all the thinking for them, hands out "material" which is the basis for quizzes and marks, and gives many A's. . . . Most of the students are really like potted plants waiting for the teacher to sprinkle them with knowledge. And then these inanimate individuals pass judgment on their teachers!

Interestingly enough, student evaluations in this case gave full credit for subject-matter competence and encouragement to thinking, but reflected the teacher's opinion of his students in low ratings on such qualities as attitude toward students, tolerance to disagreement, and personality.

Similarly, an instructor in mathematics whose ratings were uniformly discouraging, strikes back at the raters as well as at the recipients of high ratings:

I do not believe, and I'm sure I shall never believe that the opinions expressed by the students in such surveys have the slightest significance for the instructor.

Unless the teacher is completely incompetent, for example, how is it possible for a group of trigonometry students to rate their teacher's mathematical knowledge? It was my experience that the students seemed to rate highest those men who were drillmasters, grammar school pedagogues, and arrant fools spouting vapid and misty profundities. Those men who tried to make some differentiation between college and high school teaching methods seemed to get the lowest ratings.

To summarize, I might say that in my opinion the only correlation between students' opinion and teachers' ability was negative.

That the Brooklyn College student body—relatively homogeneous in socio-economic background, in political orientation, and in educational aims—is peculiarly incompetent to discriminate between good and poor teachers, is another claim. A senior member of the faculty describes the Brooklyn College student "type" in some detail:

There are numerous intangibles which I might point out to you which perhaps would negate the whole system of student ratings.

Have you taken into account the composition of our student body? By and large they are in the lower economic-social group, mostly unanimous in their views on social welfare, capitalism, trade-unionism, and such-like topics. At home they live among similarly-minded people. Few, aside from the veterans, have journeyed anywhere outside the immediate metropolitan area. Parents, in a large part, are in the same category. I have found, on asking seniors about their opinions on socioeconomic problems, that they are of their opinion still (just the same opinion they had as freshmen); their four years' study of economics, science, and what not has not in the slightest degree provided them with even a glimpse of the opposite view. How then can they be expected to weigh evidence?

In some other college with a cross-section of students from various parts of the country, from various socio-economic levels, with assorted backgrounds of political and theological and philosophical experience, a survey of student opinion might be worth something; at this college the population is far too homogeneous and biased in one direction to be truly representative of colleges as a whole.

This bias is quite well known among teachers: those of the same opinion as the students are apt to be rated higher than those of the opposite convictions.

An associate professor in social science says it succinctly:

On account of so many of our students being PINK (caps not ours) a teacher of conservative views ranks very low with them.

The homogeneity of educational goals was further stressed by an economist of many years' teaching experience:

A student body so highly motivated by vocational interests is hardly in a position to evaluate what is and what is not relevant to the material presented in a course.

Even among instructors who found the survey results useful, the students were sharply rebuked for assumed obstructionist tactics of a political nature. An historian comments that:

These boys and girls took great relish, if I may judge from their conversation and grins, in "fixing," to use their expression, their teachers! I and other teachers who are critical of their social philosophy received ratings which had little to do with realities. Emotion, not reason, played too important a part. Elsewhere than in "New Deal" Brooklyn the survey undoubtedly will be more accurate and helpful.

A teacher in the natural sciences reports indignantly:

It was called to our attention that in many instances students *ganged up* on certain teachers. . . . I believe that that type of procedure nullified many of the good results that might have been attained. The students of Brooklyn College sometimes exhibit strange criteria for judging character and integrity of those with whom they come in contact. I say this for publication.

Equally doubtful of student judgments is a professor of English, but he expressed his views more charitably:

Our students are certainly serious minded, and highly competent judged by national norms, but at times they lack the common sense and practical view that characterizes many less intellectually stimulating students.

Moreover, the question of student bias does not end here. Some professors call for ratings only by upperclassmen; others would limit it to alumni. Still others, like a professor of romance languages, would have "the teacher judged by 'A' and 'B' students who know what the work is all about."

The harsh reality, however, is that the professor cannot choose his audience. He is just as obliged to teach students of whom he disapproves as they are obliged to accept his teaching. Poor students and freshmen are also consumers of his wares. And whether or not his students are a representative sample of American collegians, they are *his* students. What they have to say, whether it be accurate or not by any other standards, is nevertheless meaningful in its own limited sphere.

Where student impression of teaching effectiveness is sought, it is entirely irrelevant to discount "some of the evaluations given my colleagues" because they "did not correspond at all to my idea of the strength or weakness of the teacher." The very fact that discrepancies exist between student and faculty opinion enhances the value of the student reaction techniques as a method for exploiting an untapped reservoir of information on the human side of the college professor's job. In the words of William R.

Wilson of Washington State University, "Only by accident will the teaching of a man ignorant of the reactions of his class be effective. . . . The view of the students may be prejudiced, mistaken, superficial, immature, but, whatever their validity, they exist and exert a powerful influence on the effectiveness of the course." [2] In this context, as was discussed in Chapter 2, the whole question of the validity of student ratings is in itself not a valid criticism. Other reactions, while questioning student competence to judge teaching ability, nevertheless took a point of view more consonant with the aims of the study:

I believe such surveys, like radio listener surveys, are useful to the people with something to sell, be it toothpaste or education, since there is everything to be gained and nothing to lose by finding out what effect you're having on the customers. But as for the absolute validity of students' opinions, I am very doubtful.

The ratings showed me some of the ways in which, regardless of who was right, I was failing to make contact with my students in the manner or degree intended.

Because of the long and continuous training required in developing teaching methods, I believe that students, owing to the inevitable lack of experience on their part in this area, are not in a position *objectively* to evaluate teacher competence. This can be adequately determined only by fellow members of a teacher's craft, i.e., by his colleagues or his head of department. At the same time, student ratings, it seems to me, are valuable as a test to discover whether the teacher's aims and techniques are effective subjectively on the receiving end. Hence these student ratings proved, in my opinion, most fruitful as an index in determining, for example, whether a teacher has succeeded in encouraging thinking, but not in such a matter as "fairness in examinations," which is colored by the student's personal reaction to his mark and further limited by lack of background in the subject.

Now and then, the professorial responses revealed that the results of the student reaction survey created feelings of anxiety or depression among faculty members. A language teacher who received ratings well above the average stated vehemently:

. . . your survey did more harm than good. It created much confusion, misunderstanding and demoralization. The students cannot benefit from such a reaction on the part of some thirty people with long experience in the teaching field.

And a professor of English with considerably poorer ratings found that "members of the staff . . . were puzzled or depressed rather than helped."

Regrettable as is this effect on teacher morale, it is only surprising that so few instructors mentioned it, for as a young social scientist explains:

Since teachers are unaccustomed to being examined by their students, there was too much ego-involvement in the ratings for them to be accepted and used objectively by the instructors. I think that studies of this kind will gradually serve to desensitize teachers regarding student criticism.

Similarly a senior professor analyzes the unavoidable emotional reaction to student ratings and probably speaks for the majority: "We who teach enjoy a large measure of protection from criticism —a condition which leaves us ill prepared to face disconcerting facts. . . . But these teacher-reactions to student opinion," he continues, "somewhat tinged emotionally though they may be, are, on the whole, salutary, for the rationalization tends to fade, but the recollection of the factors which condition effective teaching tends to survive."

The Favorable Majority. Fortunately, we need not wait for time to redeem the constructive effects of student criticism, for the bulk of Brooklyn College professors, far from being blinded by their emotions, accepted the student ratings in the spirit in which they were intended, and apparently profited by them. While most instructors' responses testified to a general re-evaluation of their teaching techniques with consequent over-all improvement in methods of instruction, a number of interesting comments particularized the areas in which modifications were intended or had already been effected. Particularly illuminating was the report of an economist who fell below the median in only two dimensions of teaching—organization of subject matter and attitude toward students. He says:

I found that the evaluations urging me to do more lecturing and use the discussion method less was due to my preconception that students were aware of the value of the discussion method as a technique of teaching. The contrary seems to be true—the habitual pattern is still that of the teacher being a pitcher that pours information down "the minds of students" instead of a participation process. I must do more explanation of my method of teaching because I am convinced that it results in a more effective learning process! . . . I am convinced that college professors particularly are poor teachers because the emphasis is on "research" and not "teaching." I am in favor of *more* of this type of student evaluation based on some preliminary preparation on the part of student and teacher.

In contrast, a speech instructor who received low scores in organization, knowledge, and explanatory ability, plans a different kind of attack:

The ratings have made me see that the speech teacher, who is interested in the improvement of the individual's speech (we have a bilingual situation) and his speech skills, is penalized on the basis of organization and knowledge of subject, because individual work seems so sketchy from the view of the group. Therefore, I shall hereafter balance theory and practice to the end of making remedial classes unified as a group and do what individual work I can get into that setup.

Given similar symptoms, both instructors made identical diagnoses, but applied completely different remedies. It remains to be seen which medicine produces the cure and whether a higher rating in organization will be worth the sacrifice of individual attention. "A more effective learning process" or the correction of speech defects certainly appears to be a more meaningful objective than higher ratings per se.

Other instructors have also decided to concentrate on one or two aspects of teaching deemed least effective by their students. "The survey confirms my suspicions that I'm weakest in 'knowledge of subject,'" says an English instructor with excellent ratings in all other qualities, "and I'm doing everything in my power to remedy that deficiency." The "make-up of examinations" will be carefully reworked by a member of the economics department who discovered from the rating sheet that the "majority of students felt (he) was too difficult" in his examinations. "Our department," says another, "held two conferences and decided to pay more attention to the validity of examinations offered to students."

A professor of classical languages was made aware of "the need to devise better methods to stimulate thinking in the students," and an economics instructor promises to "make a real effort" in the same direction. "I always felt that my teaching stimulated student thinking," he remarks, "but my rating showed that I apparently do not."

An English instructor, rated above average in all ten teaching attributes, declares earnestly:

Where my ratings seemed somewhat low, I felt the comment justified and bore it in mind thenceforth. I was new at the college and found "attitude toward students" my greatest problem. A new survey would, I trust, indicate some improvement on that particular judgment.

Another older teacher says:

My attitude toward the subject has evidently impressed my students unfavorably. I shall endeavor to correct this by urging them to give me their reasons for coming to this conclusion.

Without concentrating on any one item of the rating sheet, some faculty members made adjustments in the light of their total profile of student judgments, often in combination with the over-all analysis of the findings. One such generalized reaction to the individual reports was the necessity for presenting material that is "interesting to the student," both in content and in method of presentation. Particularly enthusiastic was a professor in the humanities, almost all of whose ratings were below average for his field. He says:

I found your report most interesting and to me, as a teacher, most valuable. Hitherto, I had no idea as to what traits in a teacher students value. I never realized how much students valued discussion of their opinions, and it is these, I know, not facts and information which are quickly forgotten and easily accessible, that are really valuable. I am one of those who believes strongly in the importance and the validity of student attitude and evaluation of a teacher. It is the student, after all, who eats the cooking, and if it does not agree with him, it can be of little use to him in any way, for the present or the future. Although at points my self-esteem was given volcanic blows, I feel that the report was most helpful, and personally, I should welcome re-evaluation every year or so. Your report was influential in changing my approach to students and my methodology. First, I was more humble and respectful of student opinion and of their contributions. Secondly, I recast my classroom teaching techniques so as to put considerably more stress on student discussion and on their exchange of points of view.

Along similar lines, an economics instructor outlines his plans for the future:

The ratings have made me aware of some of my personal shortcomings and have caused me to reorganize some of my courses and my teaching methods—to allow more discussion, more time for personal interviews for students, more time spent on questions even if somewhat irrelevant, less attention to syllabi and completing the outline, more attention to what students are interested in as a point of departure for deeper analysis.

A sociology professor, rated very successful as a teacher, nevertheless, intends to "modify courses by omitting some less important academic material." In the same department, however, another instructor reports his intention to "systematize and simplify" his approach "so that the average student can get the hang of it as well as the few exceptional ones." Despite the high premium put on encouragement to thinking by all the students of the social sciences, he concludes, "Simplification should thus tend to improve things for those who do not think but mainly learn."

Other typical responses that can be classified under the descriptive heading, "I intend to place more emphasis on teaching from the student point of view," come from all the major fields of instruction—the arts, natural science and social science. Such statements as these were frequent:

The study confirmed my feeling that the college instructor must pay attention to classroom technique, i.e., to teaching, and that he cannot rely upon the subject matter to provide its own incentive to the student.

One of the problems in teaching that shall have my attention in the future will be "presentation of class material."

The survey has given me an excellent basis for changing my presentation and for putting more emphasis on interesting students and organizing material from their point of view.

Finally, the over-all finding, says a teacher of one of the fine arts, by pointing up "some strong as well as weak points in our general field," led to the department's "entirely replanning two courses to correct, if possible, the weaknesses."

Without describing the nature of their modifications, a considerable number of the faculty gave eloquent testimony to having been generally stimulated toward eliminating or ameliorating the weak links in their teaching procedures. From the new instructor eagerly awaiting some appraisal of his effect on his students to the experienced professor brought up short by the ghost of "things I once knew were important but which I had not thought much about lately," all have one thing in common—a respect for the student's role in education, for, as an older member of the English department puts it, "By whose ultimate criteria are we teaching, if not by the students'?"

The attitude of the new teacher was expressed by an instructor in these terms:

Since I am relatively new in the teaching profession, I was eager to learn what my students thought of my efforts and to have pointed out to me deficiencies which I might not be able to observe in myself. The results of the survey have stimulated me to try to overcome the shortcomings pointed out by my students.

Another new teacher was able to secure a measure of self-confidence from the revelation of "strengths" of which he was not aware, as well as some guidance for the future. Sometimes the confidence of experienced people also needs to be bolstered, as witness the response of a language professor, who having taught

for some twenty years, says, "It was gratifying to receive good ratings and to know that what I try to do gets across to the students."
And a classicist apparently found security in criticism. "It has
stimulated me to re-thinking and changing a number of my procedures. In general, I feel that I benefited from your survey and
am grateful to you for it." Another appreciative teacher was a
professor of political science with a quarter century of educational
experience:

The survey has in a sense enabled me to see myself as my students
see me. I have carefully reflected on the ratings the students gave me in
the light of my specific methods, and content used in my courses.
Certainly with reference to one quality in which I received a lower rating than I expected, the students were probably justified, and I can
do something about improving my courses in this respect.

Similarly, a young teacher of chemistry put the student ratings
to work for him. "They show me where I'm weak and where I'm
strong and therefore indicate where I must look to strengthen
the weak points." He adds:

The essence of democracy is in a sense to know what the other man
thinks and how he criticizes you, and then to take this expression into
consideration. Teaching without criticism, as is the general rule, is
not really teaching—nor is it democratic. Criticism or self-criticism is
the way we learn. In this case it is the teacher who has to learn to
teach.

The whole idea of student ratings made a strong appeal to some
instructors as an expression of the democratic spirit. "I consider
your survey an important step in the right direction—toward a
more democratic relationship of teachers and students," comments
a social scientist. An arts professor embroiders the theme: ". . . I
think that your work is most valuable and as a man of European
background, I am really impressed by this exposition of true
democratic spirit."

Indeed, the frequent recurrence among professorial responses
of such phrases as "the student's right to judge instructors," the
"human side of teaching," and the importance of "again looking

at teaching from the other side of the fence" re-emphasizes a common factor among the large and heterogeneous group of college teachers who accepted and made the most of the student reaction survey. Whatever that common denominator is, whether personality trait or part of a whole philosophy of life, one of its essential elements is the attitude that "students are people too." And, ironically, this too is an essential element of the good teacher. The following are a few illustrative excerpts bearing on this point. A romance language instructor says:

It has proved to me that good teaching involves something more than mastery of technique or knowledge of subject matter—the human side of teaching tends to be underestimated. There must be a strong student-teacher bond for effective teaching.

A young instructor in the arts is taking precautions against forgetting that "the teacher can learn from the student as well as the reverse situation. I am vitally interested in a report of this kind because I feel that so many teachers teaching for a long time forget they are dealing with human beings. Their job is a mechanical one in which they turn out so many by-products. I don't wish to get that way and will always be anxious to know where I can improve my teaching."

Similarly, an instructor of physics commends the Rutgers survey for having called to his attention the "importance of the student as a real 'person,'" and a classical language professor says the ratings have helped him to "understand the needs of his students better" by helping to put himself "in the student's position." An instructor in education goes on:

Since teaching does not take place in a vacuum, it is always beneficial to a teacher to know what his students think of him and his teaching ability; such knowledge rounds out the picture and can lead to better teaching if the instructor has an open mind.

It would be possible to continue for pages with similar expressions. One concluding quotation, however, leaves little unsaid. It comes from a senior professor in one of the largest departments:

I find such ratings extremely useful in keeping me informed on my approach to students—and successful presentation of material. It is stupid and irrelevant to brush aside student criticism with the statement that students are not competent in evaluating the scholarly attributes of their instructors. After all, if students dislike my presentation or criticize my attitude or object to my voice, personality or mannerism, I am that much less effective as a teacher. If they believe me poorly prepared or confused or inarticulate in presenting my material, I am clearly at fault. I must establish contact with them on terms they recognize as valuable. Therefore student ratings are of value to keep me from being stuffy or complacent. The cause of dullness, lack of vitality in class presentation on the part of many college teachers is the absence of checks or criticism on the part of their audience. Such criticism as these surveys offer serve to keep a teacher from becoming immersed in subject matter, dictatorial in attitude and dead in ideas.

Such is the reaction of a single faculty to a single survey of student opinion of teaching. It is conclusive of nothing. It constitutes but fragmentary evidence. It is only part of the record. It does, however, demonstrate one thing clearly. Teachers are ready to recognize the implications of their "protected" status. The vague uneasiness with which they face the responsibilities of educating a new generation is a chronic inhibition of which they would gladly be rid. And while students can by no means provide the complete therapy, such a systematic tapping of student attitudes, on the basis of these results, appears to play a legitimate part.

11

STUDENT OPINION AND
BETTER TEACHING

BOTH the confidential ratings and the over-all analysis of student attitudes must share the credit for whatever success this effort may ultimately have in improving the quality of teaching on this particular campus. The human record of the preceding chapter strongly suggests that more satisfying classroom experiences may be anticipated. Yet it was against the background of student reactions to other instructors, and to college in general, that the individual teacher could best understand and gain insight into his own students. Through both devices an obvious gap in our knowledge of the teaching process was at least partially filled.

Over and beyond its direct utility to the immediate instructional staff concerned, however, this research into student attitudes may possibly have more general applicability. Certain broader issues have been uncovered, and suggestive data compiled. While obviously it is both dangerous and unwarranted to generalize from the specific, some of these implications are worth noting.

The Elimination of Potential Tensions. Perhaps the most suggestive clews lie in the student constructs of ideal and actual professors.

Insofar as our study has gone, the ideal professor is a multiple concept. The student visualizes his ideal in terms of the peculiar nature of the course. We have found that the physical science professor, the social science and humanities professors each possesses unique qualities *in the ideal thinking of the students.* Instead of finding *the* student image of *the* professor, we have found three more or less distinct images or constructs. The significance of this is unmistakable. Rightly or wrongly the student approaches the classroom situation with expectations not only of general instructional qualities, but with differential expectations depending on the work to be done.[1] Agreement or disagreement with the student concepts of ideal instruction is in this context irrelevant. Classroom morale can no better afford frustration on the part of the student than for the professor.

The significance of the ideal constructs is most pointed when it is considered along with actual ratings. Whereas the ideal construct varies with the type of course taught, the actual ratings of professors are much the same for the different areas of study. Although professors within each division of study showed differences in student estimation, the average ratings of professors in each area were similar on practically every attribute evaluated. While this attests a well balanced faculty, it suggests that standards of training and selection may have been too uniform, in terms of student expectation. (Certain exceptions to this have appeared, as in the instance of social science professors who rated exceptionally high on tolerance to disagreement, which to the students was a uniquely desirable attribute in this area.) The problem is particularly acute for the sciences, since in this area there is a most clearcut visualization of "ideal" instruction by the vast majority of the students. In other areas students are less homogeneous in their expectations and hence more of them will find satisfaction in a variety of outstanding qualities.

If we accept student ideals as having some relevance, then it is obvious that the very lack of variation among divisions suggests re-evaluation of criteria in professorial selection. This does not imply that students are the final judges of effective teaching, but it indicates that some criteria of effective teaching probably vary between areas of study in certain fairly well defined directions. Certainly any general movement toward the improvement of college teaching should take cognizance of these variable requirements. Such responsibility is evident unless the seasoned judgment of educators denies the relevance of the student construct. In this case we find the alternative responsibility of educating the student as to what his expectations should be in respect to instructional goals and techniques. A wholly satisfactory classroom situation would necessitate pursuit of one or the other of these alternatives.

While the general uniformity of instruction from division to division poses serious questions in educational policy, a more fundamental dilemma is found in the frequent incongruity of the student's ideal construct with his actual ratings. Notably we have found that high value is placed upon thought stimulation in social science classes by the great majority of students. But in fact the social science faculty (as for other divisions) received their lowest ratings on this quality. Similarly in science, students were in close agreement on the importance of explanatory ability, yet the scientists were notably weak on this attribute. These, and similar contrasts, unlock areas of potential classroom tension, areas which could not be reached through simple teacher evaluation alone. While on the basis of ratings we may conclude that students have judged their faculty most critically on fairness in examinations and stimulation to thinking, the dimensions of these problems are far from equal in the student's eyes. Likewise where certain other traits such as speaking ability are given low ratings, our concern cannot be so great as in those areas where students offer low evaluations on attributes which they evaluate highly, i.e., stimulation to thinking, organization of materials, and in some areas, tolerance to disagreement.

It is not within the scope of this work to attempt recommendations for resolving the incongruence of student ideals and their actual classroom observations. It is unlikely that such discrepancies will follow identical patterns in other institutions. It is also unlikely that many institutions will fail to find incongruities of similar nature. The delineation of them can offer a firm scientific foundation upon which committees or individuals can work toward the improvement of academic morale, as well as toward increasing technical instructional efficiency. Here are guide posts and clews which may stimulate efforts to improve personnel selection policy as well as providing one yardstick against which professional practice can be measured. The most crucial practical observation in this context is that a single yardstick, a single set of instructional standards, cannot realistically be applied throughout a college faculty. We have found in one American college striking differences between the applicable standards and the evaluations of reality. The tensions potentially involved in this situation are real ones, whether the students' judgments are accurate or not. The resolution of such inconsistencies will come only through intensive and localized studies of student thinking processes and of professional performance. We have found an isolated virus; research in therapeutics must follow.

Better Definition of Classroom Goals. Less directly, some of these materials indicate how students visualize the functions and ends of the classroom situation. Thus we find them defining the social science class in terms of thought stimulation, but science classes in terms of the acquisition of facts. In humanities and social sciences the notion of the classroom as a place to absorb facts appears to be less dominant. In the latter areas the classroom is a place to hear new ideas, value judgments, and to find tolerance in the expression of diverse ideas. And while the point is statistically insignificant, it is important to note that superior scholars tend to visualize even science instruction in less rigidly factual terms.

From such materials, perhaps, comes a clew of some pertinence for curricular evaluation. Certainly they might be expected to stimulate clarification of the purposes of scientific education in the college. Are we, in these students' judgments, seeing a reflection of contemporary overemphasis upon substantive knowledge in the scientific fields? Has the teaching of science itself brought forth a shallow interpretation of the science professor's role? Has some inherent difficulty in the comprehension of scientific concepts made the student thankful if he can "acquire" certain facts without the hope of going beyond? Has the very weight of actual substantive knowledge in these fields grown so that students justifiably realize a futility in attempting to go beyond "absorption" on the undergraduate level? These are questions which cut to the very roots of educational goals and the role of the classroom in their attainment.

Improving Professorial Understanding of Students. Theoretically there is no doubt but that the professor's clear understanding of student attitudes toward him is a valuable adjunct to his instructional skills. Insofar as teaching is a process of reciprocal relationships, the professor can function most effectively when he has the maximum understanding of his students' viewpoints, toward his own behavior and toward instructional goals.[2] It has been a major hypothesis of this study that the objective expression of student attitudes toward the professor himself offers direct utility to the professor in formulating his role conception and his technique.[3] The apparent validity of this hypothesis was demonstrated in the preceding chapter. While student attitudes could not feasibly be re-tested subsequent to the professor's study of his ratings, the reactions of the professors as to the utility of the ratings have been studied in some detail. And we may emphasize again that an objective of this study was not to provide college administrators with a basis for direct personnel action. All data on individual professors were held in strict confidence between the analysts and the professor concerned.[4]

It seems clear that the ultimate utility of ratings rests upon the professor's ability to grasp what is in the student's mind. This is not so simple as it may sound. Assuming a positive attitude toward the results, for a professor to know simply that students find him to be "excellent," "mediocre" or "poor" helps not at all. Some specificity in evaluations is a first requirement. But bare ratings, even in some detail, hold their major significance only when subjected to general analysis. This process can permit the professor to see himself in his position relative to his colleagues; to understand the factors influencing ratings on particular attributes; and to know the relative importance of those attributes themselves in student opinion. Student attitudes toward college instruction per se are likewise valuable data since they are subjective factors influencing judgments of concrete issues and courses. The student's conception of "ideal" instructional qualities plays a crucial role as a part of the over-all analysis, and is valuable for the insight it provides into the student's standards as he views his instructor. This is particularly important when studied in direct contrast with the actual ratings given professors. We have in this device not only a means of rendering the ratings more intelligible to the professor, but also the possibility of delimiting general areas of potential tension between student and teacher, i.e., where expectations and actuality, in the students' eyes, fail to correspond. The comparison of what the student values in *a* professor with with what he actually sees in *his* professor has broad implications for both course planning and the selection and training of faculty personnel.

Delineation of Factors Affecting Students' Judgments. Differences in the attitudes of various student body segments are also significant for an understanding of the actual ratings given professors. There is, as we have seen, widespread belief that the poor scholar down grades his professor and likewise that underclassmen are incompetent of evaluation. These preconceptions need a maximum of testing through inductive devices. Of equal importance are other variables which might reasonably hold relationship to the students' judgment—age, sex, major field, veteran status, marital status and employment experience. Obviously no single study can cover the variety of experiences and conditions responsible for student judgment, although several outstanding potential conditioners were included here—marks in the course, size of class, class in college, whether course was required or elective, and sex of student. The results have offered surprisingly little by way of significant differences in the ratings of teachers. It might reasonably have been hypothecated that objective features of the classroom situation would influence the students' evaluation of the professor. Two such factors of outstanding potential importance were studied: the size of the class and whether or not the course was required of the student. Our results confirm the results of other investigations which tend to show the unimportance of class size as a factor in professor evaluation. It seems highly probable that the student is evaluating the professor with a full recognition of the limits imposed on his behavior by the number of students with whom he must deal in a single classroom. The fact that a course is taken as a required one likewise has slight effect upon the student's judgment of the professor. While it may be assumed that the "required course" group contains a number of individuals with negative attitudes toward the course itself, such a condition has apparently not seriously biased judgments of the professor himself. There is apparently some considerable ability and willingness on the students' part to distinguish between their attitudes toward the course and toward the professor who teaches it. This was not directly ascertained but it is suggested in the data.

This investigation, like those of Remmers, Starrack and others, points a stubborn finger at the individual instructor as the most important variable in student judgments of teaching efficiency. "What the teacher is and does," says Remmers, "is from the student viewpoint the important differential between high and low ratings." [5] Neither maturity, nor ability, nor the size of the class were found to have any significant effect on the ratings of instructors.

The present survey, however, although reinforcing the earlier findings in these particular respects, discovered an interesting relationship between student grades and reactions to instructors. While it should be emphasized that the differences between ratings of poor and good students were in most cases very slight, at the same time the consistency of the relationship cannot be denied. It has been evident that the inferior scholar looks with more critical eyes upon his professor. This is particularly true in his evaluation of fairness in examinations and in professor's attitude toward the student. On the other hand poor scholars and superior ones differed little in their evaluation of professorial subject matter competence and in no notable manner in their ratings of speaking ability, or attitude toward subject. There has certainly been no evidence that inferior students displayed any general tendency to down grade a professor arbitrarily due to spite. And although inferior scholars were more critical in general, all scholarship groups were in general agreement on the ranking of their instructors' strong and weak points. It is reasonable to interpret the effect of class standing as having only a limited biasing effect, and then only in the evaluation of attributes most closely related to the professors' grading judgment. Far from invalidating the over-all results of ratings, the grade bias appears to be a sincere and largely conscious projection of specific incompetences upon the instructor. We have found surprisingly slight reflections of over-all antipathy and willful villification of a professor by a low grade student. Student rationalization is evidenced certainly by the down rating of the professor in fairness, attitude and explanatory ability, but there is no evidence that low grading makes for a total rejection of a professor by the student concerned. On the other hand we have noted a slight tendency toward the halo effect in the ratings of superior scholars. While the evidence is not definitive, the great variability of ratings upon different attributes by superior scholars (as well as inferior) indicates no general uncritical acceptance of "the easy grader." [6] These observations fit closely with the findings of other researches and from a quite different approach validate the observations of Remmers, Cole and others as to objectivity in student judgment. The recognition of areas in which grade bias is felt can add a new dimension to the observations of these writers. And it should be recognized that we must expect the experiences of a student to influence his judgment. Subjective valuations should not be upheld as objective reality. We may, however, by the study of subjective valuations by different groups and from different angles come toward an understanding of the practical, tangible classroom situation.

Providing Clews to "Good Teachers." Quite as important, both for theory and for educational administration, as the evaluation of professors by students, is the delineation of the professorial types eliciting various kinds of student responses. Who, in objective and descriptive terms, is the successful teacher in the students' eyes? Beyond the direct significance of our findings to the institution concerned, the results offer hypotheses worth testing.

While it was impossible, in the scope of the survey, to make a study of all faculty characteristics relevant to the attitudes of the students, certain pertinent data were collected. These offer interpretative background to the individual professor, but perhaps of greater import is the fact that the potentially disturbing effects of conditions normal to the conventional college organization can be laid bare: wide age distribution, various levels of training, etc. Several of these variables are uniquely significant since they themselves, as measures or symbols of academic attainment (degrees and rank), imply levels of instructional achievement. It is reasonable that they be tested against the weight of student judgment.

The question of research activity, for example, is a constantly recurring one. Are productive scholars necessarily the best teachers? Again, keeping in mind that student judgments are to be

viewed within a narrow framework, there is a suggestive relationship between a professor's research activity and his students'
estimates of him as a teacher. More work needs to be done on this
point.

While academic rank, higher degrees, and other objective characteristics are all relevant at various levels, perhaps the most disconcerting relationship has to do with age. Younger teachers, with
few exceptions, rank higher in student estimates. Although older
and more experienced teachers are generally regarded as "knowing
their stuff," their younger colleagues are looked upon as more successful on other counts.

This finding, if borne out in further researches, has negative
significance to the frequently heard suggestion in support of some
master-apprentice system or, at least, a minimum facility for
offering guidance and counsel to younger teachers. If the older
men are, in fact, better teachers, then it is evident that they are not
utilizing their abilities or that students are not recognizing them.
We cannot, of course, be sure of the extent to which this situation is unique, but the problem is sufficiently serious to warrant
testing in other educational communities. At this stage, theoriz-
ing as to the causal factors involved would be little more than
speculation. The possibilities range from suggestions that older
men can permit themselves to lapse into routine performances,
to the claim that their time is more encroached upon by non-
teaching obligations. It is interesting, in this connection, that this
age factor has received some recognition by college administrators.
In a study of 291 deans, 79 per cent considered the presence of
"rusty" teachers a serious liability and were more concerned with
the question of older teachers than with that of inexperienced
ones.[7]

Were such a relationship to be validated, the implications for
higher education would be far-reaching indeed, but, on a different
level, any determinative power exerted by such variables as age or
research experience should have *some* bearing upon personnel assignment, and possibly training. Once again, this does not imply

that student judgments are objectively accurate, but simply that student attitude is one concrete element in effective instruction.

More Adequate Understanding of Students' Educational Motivation. In order for the professor to evaluate his techniques and gain the maximum from his class, it is essential that the maximum be known regarding the interests, purposes and criticisms of the college in general. Full understanding of the student's viewpoint is impossible but certain key responses can be ascertained which offer help in "sizing up" the general thinking of the student regarding his college education. This is particularly useful when the differences are studied between different segments of the student body. While the specific content of these attitudes will undoubtedly vary from campus to campus, certain of the differences and lack of difference in the attitudes of various segments of the student body offer provocative insights that may have some more general validity.

Thus we have found that the majority of students have been primarily motivated toward college with direct or indirect vocational incentives. The majority, however, are strongly enough bent upon a college career that they would have rejected an "interesting job at sixty-five dollars a week" in order to continue. The common student objection to "too many required courses" is voiced by only about one-half of the students, and nearly as high a proportion found the balance between specialized training and general education satisfactory.

We may judge that in general we have here a student body looking upon their college career with strong practical eyes, but nevertheless very much aware of its general cultural value. In view of the vocational bent of the majority there is relatively little criticism of general education requirements. This condition has only limited bearing upon the problems of effective teaching beyond the confines of the college studied. However, certain of the variations and lack of variations within the student body raise stimulating issues of broader significance. Students of high scholarship, women, and upperclassmen were more strongly motivated toward college education, had less direct vocational incentive, and were better satisfied with the degree of specialization and general requirements which they found. On the other hand, it is of considerable significance that veterans and nonveterans were practically identical in their attitudes on those issues, suggesting the possibility that educators have exaggerated the differential character of the veteran as a college enrollee. Sex and scholastic standing made far greater difference on these issues than does the fact of military service. Similarly we find that identification with college life through high participation in extracurricular activities has little influence upon incentives toward college and judgment of the curricular balance. Only in rare instances did the major course pursued by the student reflect variations in student thinking on these matters.

The testing and validation of these relationships on a wide scale could provide valuable generalizations for the guidance of educational policy. It is clear that differences in educational motivation provide different viewpoints from which the students evaluate their courses and define their personal educational needs. At the most elemental level such data point out the segments within a student body most in need of enlightenment as to the broader purposes of higher education. Although simple progression within the academic environment appears to broaden the student viewpoint, it is readily conceivable that this educational process could be speeded through the use of validated generalizations regarding the groups likely to present such problems.

To conclude, it is our feeling that the primary value of this volume will not lie in its validation or qualification of sociological or educational principles. To lay down broad scientific generalizations has not been our objective. It is certain that findings derived from the study of a single college campus cannot have claim to general validity. No American college is typical of American colleges. However it is obvious that many of our objectives and our findings are relevant to the establishment of generalizations.

Whether or not further researches validate our observations on a broad basis, we believe that at this stage many implications of the inquiry have a vital bearing upon the central problems of college instruction.

12

New Avenues of Research

THE favorable professorial response to this project does not mean, of course, that any final answer to the very complex problem of measuring student-faculty relationships has been found. The perfect questionnaire has not been constructed, nor is the technique for handling the results guaranteed to extract the last drop of information. Beneath the surface of student opinion lies a wealth of unexplored material, as, for example, the reasons behind student attitudes. Many such interesting and potentially productive areas of research were recognized from the beginning, but had to be sacrificed on the altar of budgetary and other practical considerations.

The area of this study has been closely limited. Within the field of social relations we have studied relationships between professors and students. Within this relationship we have studied *one* subjective dimension, the student's image of his professor. And even in this narrow range of inquiry it is readily apparent that the practical exigencies of a research operation permit no elaborate exploration. We have hued closely to a particular technique and have dealt largely in the quantitative treatment of qualitative factors. The professorial image which we inevitably find is more a congerie or complex of elements than an organic, dynamic whole. To fill out the construct of the professor into a living image, it would be necessary to supplement the objective statistical techniques with intensive interviews. We have sampled the student's thinking rather than encompassed it.

Intensive Interviewing of Students. The desirability of following up such a statistical inquiry with further qualitative materials is unquestionable. If our method provides a construction of the arms, legs, head and torso of the professor, depth interviewing focused to that end will bring those features into organic unity. The value of such an additional approach does not end here. Only through such additional material can we understand fully just how the student defines the attributes upon which he rates a professor. What does the student see in tolerance to disagreement, in stimulation to thinking? Does he in the latter instance mean challenge to go beyond or does he mean professorial agreement with his personal values, i.e., approval of the professor's stimulation of *other* people's thinking? Or does he mean, as a history professor suspects, stimulation to emotional expression? The full significance of student evaluations will not come without inquiry into such difficult aspects of the problem.

The frequency and the urgency with which instructors request assistance in interpreting the rating sheet and in visualizing themselves from the student's side of the looking glass heavily underscores the need for intensive research into what the student has in mind. In the words of one instructor, the bare statistical interpretation has, in many cases, only furnished a "necessary shot in the arm." To the instructor who is jolted out of his lethargy into facing "weaknesses I once knew were there but have long since forgotten," and to another who was awakened to the fact that he "wasn't getting away with anything," the way is clear. But take the not unfamiliar case of the teacher who is shocked into the realization that he has failed to establish contact with his students on the very level toward which he has constantly striven. In his own eyes, he is not a teacher of facts, but rather a man whose destiny it is to open new vistas for his students, to inspire the young people in his classes to a fuller appreciation and development of their capacities. "I have never regarded my students as mere ciphers," he declares.

In the eyes of his students, however, he is precisely that which he thought he was not and for which he often and bitterly excoriated his colleagues. His students have dealt him a harsh blow and given him no explanation. He can't step through the looking glass, but his students, if they were asked, might give him a fair description of what the other side looks like.

The disappointed and bewildered professor is not alone, for the demand for clarification of some of the descriptive terms used in the questionnaire "to insure that they be understood in the same way by each student," as well as the cry for more free comments, came from several quarters. The most extreme illustration of the need for greater detail or more assistance in interpretation of the data was the case of a young instructor in chemistry, who was rated in the lowest quartile on all attributes of good teaching. "This report has checked what I have sensed about myself as a teacher," he admits, "but I am sorry to say that it has given me no solution to the problems of teaching."

Other instructors, while finding themselves in happier straits, were none the less convinced of the practical necessity for a more complete statement of student opinion. According to a young philosopher:

I think they (the ratings) would be more useful, though obviously also more cumbersome, if more detailed. For example, if one speaks poorly, why does he? If one is unfair, why? and so on. The results of this test were personally not as useful to me as those I conduct for myself, in which students express their opinions informally.

Along similar lines, a teacher of social science observes:

If the students had been allowed to elaborate their judgments of individual teachers, I think the survey would have been more valuable than a mere quantitative, statistical percentile interpretation of the data, although this would introduce a complex qualitative element into students' criteria of judgment.

An experienced professor of political science also found the individual rating too indefinite for practical guidance, although her students' reports pointed up a sharply defined pattern of excellence in transmitting subject matter, but a lack of sympathetic attention to students. "Frankly," she avers, "the report affected my teaching but slightly. The statistics simply state facts with little indication in the nature of constructive criticism. . . . Perhaps the classifications were not detailed enough."

The possibility of an easy remedy to the lack of clarity in questionnaire items was suggested by a veteran member of the faculty who remarked that "most of the teachers did not know what questions were asked. Perhaps if they had, the answers would have been more intelligible." The statements at the various points on the student evaluation scales were, in fact, highly descriptive and might have served in some instances to bring into clearer focus the somewhat blurred outlines of the professorial characteristics being measured. This, however, is obviously no solution for the young instructor who wants to know "why" he is failing to make contact with his students. There is no denying the value of more intensive qualitative investigation. While such a research effort may not necessarily solve all of the problems of teaching, it is heartening that college instructors demand it.

More Detail in Reporting the Results. Hand in hand with the desire for more detail in the questionnaire items is the request by faculty members for more detail in the reports of individual ratings, particularly with respect to student characteristics. The practical problems involved in furnishing such data only partially reflected limitations in the research budget. In too many instances the number of student opinions upon which the rating was based was too small to allow such statistical breakdowns as sex, age, class in college, grades, etc. The results could have been nothing but misleading.

It was hoped that the over-all analysis of student ratings would restore some of the vitality and individuality to the summarized confidential reports. That this objective was achieved is evidenced by the general tone of satisfaction in the faculty response. The point of view of some few instructors who would have welcomed more specific identification of the sources of student opinion is, nevertheless, understandable. Occasionally an instructor feels that the high and low points of his teaching were smoothed out to a meaningless plateau of "median" student ratings. He feels frustrated in not being able to trace the effects of his teaching beyond the average student; the concept of a student type is an abstraction not easily grasped. And then, he is asked to apply the recommendations of this abstraction to the concrete classroom situation of good and poor students, of freshmen and seniors, of men and women who hang on his every word, and others whose presence hangs on the word of the faculty scholarship committee. He feels justified in demanding to know from what specific materials his final score was derived. A young science instructor reacts vigorously to the idea of a repetition of the survey partly because "the raw data for the instructors' own students are much more revealing than the summarized results which tend to conceal much that is pertinent." A philosophy instructor suggests, but without vehemence, that "It might be interesting to teachers to know whether their students were substantially agreed or whether the percentage conclusion was the average of unusually divergent opinions." A professor of education apparently finds the generalized findings on elective and required courses no substitute for specific information on *her* students.

Since the data submitted did not differentiate between the values of students who took courses as electives and those who took the course as part of the required sequence, it is difficult to determine just what percentage of the final rating reflects each point of view.

The generalized case for a separation of ratings according to courses was ably argued by several members of the faculty. A social scientist reports:

I should like to have a record of the courses in which the students had contact with the instructor. For example, if an instructor receives a particular rating with respect to a given trait, he is curious to know whether he rendered that impression consistently in all of his classes, or whether these ratings came only from students in a particular course.

And an English instructor puts it this way:

In general, I know my strengths and weaknesses. I am not so much interested in having my attention drawn to them as I am in learning how I am going over in *one* class—where I am trying very hard—in contrast to a class where I have "eased off" because of over-work or the time of day.

On the other hand, several requested some over-all appraisal of teaching effectiveness. A teacher in the humanities even suggests a technique for measuring his total impression on the students:

I should like to know how many of the students, who have had a course with me, would take it again, if they could go back in time to the day they chose my section and were faced with the same choice again.

All such comments and requests seem reasonable enough. To fulfill them presents the researcher with some taxing problems, but at least some of the issues which are at stake would appear to justify the effort.

This is not to say, however, that much of additional value could not be gleaned from such materials as are now in hand from the present study. Some considerable experimental analysis yet remains to be done. While, for example, there appeared to be no significantly biasing effect in the halo surrounding a student's conception of an individual teacher, a more exhaustive factor analysis of what characteristics tend to cling together may well pay rich dividends in exposing from the student point of view instructional strengths and weaknesses. It might even be possible to delineate certain types of student responses and thus provide rating recipients with further insights into their teaching methods. Whether or not such research will "solve" teaching problems becomes irrelevant. Solutions, however, should logically follow from better understanding.

Analysis of the Professorial Personality. In view of the "atomistic" presentation of the professor, the request for an appraisal of the teaching effectiveness of the whole man is justified. We have fragmentized the professor into ten attributes of good teaching. Perhaps he should be put together again with some new cohesive materials. An intensive study of the personality components of selected high and low rating professors might offer more illumination than the correlation analysis of more objective traits with teaching ability.

What is good teaching personality? Is there any relationship between student approval and the degree of introversion-extroversion, submission-dominance, etc., as measured by standardized tests? Or does the special magic that makes a great teacher scorn objective measurement?

Even the most energetic quantifiers cannot fail to admit that teachers are human beings and not merely a bundle of pedagogical characteristics. Social psychology has unraveled many of the mysteries of the human personality, but there is much yet to learn. If the concept of teaching—a two-way process of interpersonal relations—which we have emphasized throughout this work is correct, then the imponderables are certainly important. The charge that a rating scale fails to measure the *art* of teaching is correct.

Among the numerous eulogies of great teachers are tributes to all kinds of "objective" men—the wise men, the young and old men, the lame, the halt and the blind. But the common denominator, the spark which can ignite a flame in others, has not yet been identified. An interesting experiment which could conceivably give substance to some of the intangibles in the problem might involve the selection by students of their conceptions of the world's great teachers, their reasons for the selection, and finally their judgment as to where their own teachers have failed or where they have come up to the ideal.

We have, in short, based our case on ten pillars of teaching excellence. We are not, however, sure that these are the only criteria. Nor are we certain that some ingredient in the cement which binds them together does not, after all, make the difference between good teaching and bad.

Professorial Conceptions of Educational Goals. The professor's functioning has been reconstructed by his clients. Our interest has been, almost exclusively, from the students' point of view. This single approach, however studious, does not necessarily cover all dimensions of the professorial role. It would be advantageous, for example, were supplementation made in terms of the professor's conception of his own functioning. And of further pertinence might be an evaluation of the professor by a disinterested objective observer. The professor's self evaluation could be readily obtained and significant insights into teaching problems should be had in its comparison with student evaluations. More difficult to achieve would be the third evaluation, that of the objective observer, which raises difficult problems in the determination of "objectivity" and in the practical issue of holding the normal classroom constant under such a period of observation.

In like manner the faculty judgments as to the highest attributes in teaching in their fields should afford useful comparison with student judgments. This utility would be enhanced if some consensus of scholars on the issues could be entered into the comparative study. Such a procedure could offer a substantial groundwork for clarification of teaching goals, and could have profound implications when studied in the light of actual evaluations by the student, the teacher himself and the outside observer.

Although no systematic attempt was made to probe into the professor's conception of his own role, some faculty reactions to the survey hinted strongly at a serious conflict between professorial and student conceptions of teaching goals. Among the opponents of various aspects of the survey itself—particularly of student competence to judge instructors—was a group of professors who might have been cut out of a single pattern, so similar were their student reaction profiles. Characteristically rated well above average in subject matter competence as well as in technical communicative skills, they made a poor record on those attributes most deeply rooted in personality traits: attitude toward students, encouragement to thinking, tolerance to disagreement, and others. It takes little imagination to reconstruct this professorial type and to understand his chagrin. His failure is certainly not one of too little endeavor. He is undoubtedly among the most conscientious of workers. He has failed to live up to his students' ideal simply because he has set his sights on another target.

If student constructs, however, are at least partially justified in terms of accepted educational functions, there is a direct implication that specialized criteria of teacher selection in the different academic areas is justified. Congruity between the student ideal expectation and its realization in actual professors cannot be achieved through universal standards of teacher selection and training. Equally apparent is the implication that the solution to tensions arising from frustrations so generated will not lie in inculcating prospective college teachers with certain pedagogical techniques. These ideal roles represent basic differences in the way the professor visualizes the total classroom instructional process, its goals and its methods. The acquisition of a strictly pedagogical technology may make for better teaching generally, but it would be helpless before the problem posed in the discrepancy between ideal and actual roles. We are dealing here with what is likely to be basic personality patterns and certainly differential concepts of professorial functioning. Conformity with student constructs presumes basic differences between natural and social scientists, not so much in technique as in definition of the instructional role and the very ends toward which classroom behavior is to be oriented. More intensive study will undoubtedly indicate that the differences in student images are more complex than those we describe here. Not only does this phenomenon need further study, but also a more detailed classification of professorial fields.

The Need for Replication. Finally, it is essential that the study of teacher-student relationships be extended in various types of institutions if such research is to rest upon scientific foundations. It is not enough that the unique relationships in a particular college be probed. In the long run the clarification of educational goals, the reduction of tensions, and improvement of teaching effectiveness will rely upon generalized principles of student-teacher relationships. These can be derived only through comparative analysis of studies performed in widely varying educational institutions.

The implications of this study to be sure are serious and the case for continued research with a view to confirming or repudiating their general applicability scarcely needs to be argued. If, in one institution after another, students fail to receive from the arts and social science professor the encouragement they seek to overreach themselves, while at the same time, the natural science instructor fails to give the clear explanations they seek of scientific phenomena; if college professors all over the United States tend to shrink in stature as teachers and to grow with the years only in scholarly ability, then the foundations upon which the whole system of higher education rests is made of paper. A number of faculty members astutely saw the implications of the proposal to repeat the survey in other institutions as a validating technique. A full professor in economics, for example, considered a repetition of the survey in another institution more a means of "verifying student attitudes" than of "rating instructors." A young physics instructor concurs with the statement that "the value of the survey is limited by the validity of the results." And other cryptic admonitions focus on the same point. "The broader the base, the firmer the conclusions." "The wider the sampling, the more meaningful the research."

Curiously, the unique character of Brooklyn College—urban, publicly supported, and homogeneous in composition of student body—prompted some to demand new surveys in similar colleges and others to recommend future research in dissimilar institutions.

On the one hand, an English instructor believed the value of the present survey "will be enhanced by the opportunity to compare your findings at our institution with the reactions of students of more diverse backgrounds than our fairly homogeneous student body." In like vein, a professor of sociology suggests that "it would be interesting to discover whether Brooklyn student reactions are like those of others whose social backgrounds are markedly different."

On the other hand, a convincing argument is made that further research would be most valuable if conducted in "close to uniform" institutions, "so that accurate comparisons between schools would be possible." "Comparisons with municipal institutions in other parts of the U.S.A. would be suitable. I do not believe that comparison should be made with small, privately endowed institutions."

Another kind of verification concerns the individual ratings. More interested in the personal evaluations than in the broader implications of the over-all analysis, a number of the faculty members requested a repetition of the study either to measure the extent of self-improvement resulting from the first study or merely to verify the original student judgment. Typical of the latter point of view are such statements as these:

Many factors tend to influence the results of *one* such rating. Personally I would have more faith in the ratings which I received (including those in which I ranked in the highest quartile) if the ratings represented an average of student evaluations of my teaching abilities and attitudes over a period of terms.

I think the study was quite valuable and believe that it will be more valuable if it is continued. If we had three or four such studies on ourselves, we would know better how to act upon such information.

The only way that the validity of student opinion can be established would seem to be another similar study in the near future that would act as a check upon the earlier one. I am confident that if another study produced about the same results, it would be increasingly effective in changing the teaching methods used by some of us.

Another technique for determining the extent to which an instructor should be guided by the recommendations of his students was suggested by a few serious-minded instructors who were curious about the long-term effects of classroom instruction on students. "As I look back after twenty years," says one teacher, "I can better appreciate my professors than when I was in the school, and my judgment while a student about my professors was often immature. . . ." In this connection, the value of comparing the judgments of alumni with those of an instructor's current students should prove to be a fruitful occupation, even if the results should merely show that student opinions of instructors do not change with increased maturity.

In a sense, the measurement of alumni reactions to instruction is on a different research level from the study of teacher-student relations, and is perhaps closer to the heart of all educational objectives, i.e., effecting such long-term results in individuals as those enumerated by a professor of social science who called for the extension of the scope of the study to include not only "the teacher's personal attributes and professional equipment, but also . . . the permanent effects of the teacher's instruction as the student assesses them." Particularly interested in the implications of student evaluations and the improvement of the methodology, the professor continues:

The stimulation of enduring interest, the modification of outlook and attitudes, the acquisition of operational skills—each of these as well as the all-important item of encouragement to thinking should be included in a questionnaire that invites appraisal of the competence of teachers.

But this investigation from the beginning was confined to only one ingredient which goes into making an excellent teacher and a well-rounded and educated individual, the relationship between teacher and student. Within the limits of this one component, the most dramatic and conclusive test of all, entirely in keeping with the purposes of the study, is the extent of self-improvement of faculty members. And this can best be tested by repeating the survey among the current students of those instructors who have already been tested. A professor of science speaks for a number of his colleagues:

I believe another survey should be conducted at Brooklyn within four years, so that those being rated can see if they are making any headway insofar as improvement is concerned.

But apart from all future researches which may or may not corroborate the observations of this case study, the basic issues reflected in our conclusions are actually or potentially present in every American college. The results are mainly significant in that they define areas of possible tension, trends of a disturbing nature, and at the same time offer substantive and methodological leads for clarification and further study. No college is typical of American colleges, but all participate within a common framework of cultural standards and definitions of roles for both student and teacher. While unique situational determinants will color the specific manifestations of these instructional processes, the cores of the processes themselves arise from the basic idea and structure of higher education.

Concluding Note. One of the shibboleths of contemporary society with respect to many social problems is "This is a job for education." Yet it is patent that *education,* in and of itself, will solve nothing. Our faith in the institution, particularly at the college level, borders on the magical. A college degree is a kind of touchstone to economic prosperity. It contains intrinsic properties as a kind of social necessity. This aura of importance takes on startling proportions when viewed against the confusions and uncertainties surrounding current conceptions of educational goals. We are all too ready to "leave it to education," but reluctant to assess just what it is that's going to do the job.

This volume has attempted only a small part of this assessment. It has probed into one aspect of the learning process. It has suggested some shattering hypotheses. Perhaps we had better not leave it to education.

Here, then, is a question for sound thinking and constructive effort. Depending upon how urgently we regard the issues of educating the next generation, such effort will be made. The research demands, however, currently imposed in the direction of further knowledge of our natural environment conflict with and often threaten our efforts toward better and more efficient human relations. That we know so little of the latter and so much of the former is the chronic shock. However much this limited exploration into the vital process whereby wisdom is handed down from one generation to the next may ultimately be modified, extended or generalized, it constitutes its small part toward righting the scales.

Notes

CHAPTER I

1. J. Barzun, *Teacher in America,* Little Brown & Co., Boston, 1945, p. 9.
2. F. Payne and E. W. Spieth, *An Open Letter to College Teachers,* The Principia Press, Bloomington, Ind., 1935, p. 29.
3. Barzun, *op. cit.,* p. 187.
4. The President's Commission on Higher Education, *Higher Education for American Democracy,* Vol. 1, p. 62, Washington, D.C., 1947.
5. R. F. Butts, *The College Charts Its Course,* McGraw-Hill Co., 1939, pp. 265–66.
6. The President's Commission on Higher Education, *op. cit.,* p. 62.
7. Butts, *op. cit.,* p. 357.
8. Logan Wilson (*The Academic Man,* Oxford University Press, New York, 1942, p. 103), notes that over one-half of American college teachers are in colleges having faculties of two hundred or over.

CHAPTER 2

1. Franz Schneider, *More Than An Academic Question,* The Pestalozzi Press, Berkeley, California, 1945, p. 115.
2. See Logan Wilson, *The Academic Man,* Oxford University Press, 1942, p. 188.
3. Logan Wilson, *op. cit.,* p. 178.
4. The question of whether research activity is conducive to more effective teaching is a moot point and probably depends both upon the type of research and the level of teaching, as well as the professor's personality. The findings of this study, however, suggest an interesting relationship. See Ch. 9.
5. N. Foerster, *The Humanities and the Common Man,* University of North Carolina Press, 1946, pp. 45–46.
6. Barzun, *op. cit.,* p. 195.

CHAPTER 3

1. Russell M. Cooper, "A Rising Concern for Good Teaching," *What the Colleges Are Doing,* Ginn & Co., Jan., 1950, p. 2.

2. Patterson, "An Experiment in Supervising College Teaching," *School and Society*, 21:146.
3. *New York Times*, March 22, 1949.
4. "Report of the Committee on College and University Teaching," *Bulletin of the AAUP*, XIX: 5, section 2, p. 22, May, 1933.
5. W. R. Wilson, "Scales for Supervision," *Journal of Higher Education*, 3:75–82, 1932.
6. H. H. Remmers, "Student Rating of College Teaching—A Reply," *School and Society*, 30:233.
7. R. J. Clinton, "Qualities College Students Desire in College Instructors," *School and Society*, 32:702.
8. W. A. Boussfield, "Student Ratings of Qualities Considered Desirable in College Professors," *School and Society*, 51:253–56.
9. *Ibid.*
10. The studies from which the data on qualities of teaching were assembled are reported in the following sources:
    W. A. Boussfield, *op. cit.*
    F. S. Breed, "A Guide for College Teaching," *School and Society*, 24:82–87.
    R. J. Clinton, *op. cit.*
    C. O. Davis, "Our Best Teachers," *School Review*, 34:754–59.
    D. S. Geyer, "Qualities Desired in College," *School and Society*, 63:270–71.
    E. R. Guthrie, "Evaluation of Faculty Service," *Bulletin of the AAUP*, XXXI: 255–262.
    L. W. Johnson, "The Quality of College Teaching," *Journal of Higher Education*, 13:428–33.
    C. L. Odom, "An Objective Determination of the Qualities of a Good College Teacher," *Peabody Jour. of Ed.*, 2:111.
    H. Patterson, *op. cit.*, pp. 146–47.
    A. Y. Reed, *The Effective and Ineffective College Teacher*, American Book Co., New York, 1935, p. 21.
    H. H. Remmers, "The College Professor as the Student Sees Him," *Studies in Higher Education XI*, Purdue University, March, 1929.
    A. A. Smith, "What is Good College Teaching?" *Journal of Higher Education*, 15:216–18.
    J. A. Starrack, "Student Rating of Instruction," *Journal of Higher Education*, 5:288–90.
11. A. A. Smith, *op. cit.*, p. 216.
12. Remmers, *op. cit.*, pp. 44–45.
13. *Ibid.*
14. H. H. Remmers, L. Hadley, and J. K. Long, "Learning Effort and Attitude as Affected by Class Size in Beginning College Mathematics," *Purdue Studies in Higher Education, XIX*, vol. 32, no. 9.
15. An instructor was rated higher by small groups 53 per cent of the time.
16. Starrack, *op. cit.*, p. 89.
17. Stalnaker and Remmers, "Can Students Discriminate Traits Associated with Success in Teaching?" *Journal of Applied Psychology*, Dec. 1928, pp. 602–10.
18. H. H. Remmers, "The College Professor as the Student Sees Him," *Studies in Higher Education, XI*, Purdue University, March, 1929.
19. Starrack, *op. cit.*, p. 90.
20. Remmers, *op. cit.*, p. 18.
21. Starrack, *op. cit.*, p. 90.

22. E. R. Guthrie, "Measuring Student Opinion of Teacher," *School and Society,* 25:175–76, 1927.
23. F. S. Breed, "Factors Contributing to Success in College Teaching," *Journal of Educational Research,* 16:247–53.
24. W. R. Wilson, "Students Rating Teachers," *Journal of Higher Education,* 3:79–81.
25. Patterson, "An Experiment in Supervising College Training, *School and Society,* 21:146–47.
26. Starrack, *op. cit.,* p. 89.
27. L. Cole, *op. cit.,* pp. 572, 573, 577.
28. Barzun, *op. cit.,* p. 43.
29. Sir John Adams, *The Teacher's Many Parts,* John Deach, Jr., Los Angeles, 1932, p. 196.

CHAPTER 4

1. Abraham S. Goodhartz, "Student Attitudes and Opinions Relating to Teaching at Brooklyn College," *School and Society,* Vol. LXVII, No. 1769, Nov. 20, 1948.

CHAPTER 5

1. Further insight along this approach was had by study of Houston Peterson's *Great Teachers Portrayed by Those Who Studied Under Them,* Rutgers University Press, 1946; J. McT. Daniel, *Excellent Teachers, Their Qualities and Qualifications,* University of South Carolina, 1944; and Luella Cole, *The Background of College Teaching,* Farrar & Rinehart, 1940, pp. 572–89.
2. Even to ask of *"irritating* mannerisms" is a dangerous specific form of personality inquiry, since the possession of many mild mannerisms not positively pleasing to the student might well bring forth a strong minus mark for a professor who actually irritated little or not at all. As a specific, the attribute simply does not appear to be *systematically* relevant, and at best is a perfectly negative approach—perfection is the absence of irritation.
3. Both intensive questioning and pre-testing of the questionnaire was carried out on the Rutgers campus rather than at Brooklyn College.
4. This decision was substantiated subsequently in interviews with Brooklyn College students regarding possible confusions and indecisions in their ratings.

CHAPTER 6

1. This assumption is not strictly accurate but it was not feasible in the inquiry to use a more refined classification.
2. It is recognized that valuations are inevitably present whether given conscious expression or not, so in a sense we are dealing with an hypothetical case. This is not a serious defect, however, when such a technique is used simply to get direction of desired emphasis.

CHAPTER 8

1. Butts, *op. cit.,* p. 314.
2. John Dewey, *Experience and Education,* The Macmillan Co., New York, 1938, pp. 77–78.

CHAPTER 9

1. Nicholas Murray Butler, *Scholarship and Service,* Charles Scribner's Sons, New York, 1921, p. 119.

CHAPTER 10

1. According to the report of the President's Commission on Higher Education, "The case for student evaluation of instruction as a means for improving teaching excellence is a strong one. Most theoretical objections to it vanish when practical try-out is made; faculty acceptance is typically favorable." *Higher Education for American Democracy,* Vol. 14, p. 47, 1947.
2. W. R. Wilson, "Students Rating Teachers," *Journal of Higher Education,* 3:79, 1932.

CHAPTER 11

1. More intensive study might reveal other differences in student images depending upon factors not studied here. For example, it would be advantageous to compare, within the humanities, the foreign language teacher with the professor of literature.
2. Other student attitudes are also relevant, i.e., attitude toward the subject matter of the course, but are excluded from consideration here.
3. Other investigators have found that similar evaluations have had significant effects upon instruction. See Cole, *op. cit.,* pp. 589–92.
4. It seems obvious that student ratings of instructors are only one phase of any over-all evaluation of a professor's competence. Even under the most adequate safeguards of professorial rights, the conditions under which such evaluations would be a reasonable basis for administrative action would be stringent indeed. Far greater amounts of interpretive data should be had and the ratings should be systematically applied over a period of years. It, further, would be a gross misuse of a valuable research tool if it stimulated a crude professorial catering to popularity.
5. H. H. Remmers, *The College Professor as the Student Sees Him,* Purdue Studies in Higher Education, XI, 1929, p. 52.
6. See Chapter 7.
7. Anna Y. Reed, *The Effective and Ineffective College Teacher,* American Book Co., 1935, p. 20.

APPENDIX

Form A of the questionnaire used in the Student Reaction Survey at Brooklyn College is reproduced below. Form B is omitted since it merely repeats, for four additional instructors, the rating scale (items 1–13) of Part III in Form A. As was explained in Chapter 5, Form B supplied the material for confidential reports to the individual instructors. The single rating in Form A, on the other hand, was studied for its general implications, and relationships were sought with data collected elsewhere in the questionnaire. It is on the analysis of Form A that the major findings of this book are based.

BROOKLYN COLLEGE
STUDENT REACTION SURVEY

Conducted by
Department of Sociology, Rutgers University

HOW DID THIS SURVEY COME ABOUT? *The idea of obtaining student opinion concerning teachers and college teaching in general arose with your own student body. The idea was accepted by the faculty and administration. You are now asked to give your opinion.*

WHO IS DOING THE SURVEY? *The Department of Sociology of Rutgers University, as an outside research agency, was asked to do the job. This group is engaged in social research in various fields.*

HOW WERE THE QUESTIONNAIRES SET UP? *No one has ever devised a perfect questionnaire. These forms have been designed and pre-tested over a period of many weeks. Within the limits of the budget, they are as complete and as balanced as possible.*

WHO IS PAYING FOR THE SURVEY? *The Carnegie Corporation became interested in the project and appropriated funds to cover the costs.*

HOW WILL THE RESULTS BE USED? *Needless to say, YOUR OPINIONS ARE COMPLETELY ANONYMOUS. They can in no way be connected with you personally. Two types of reports will be issued. One will be addressed to Brooklyn College as a whole and will contain the over-all findings. In addition, individual reports will be sent directly from the Rutgers office to the various faculty members.*

HOW CAN YOU HELP? *Follow the instructions* carefully. *Give us an* honest expression *of your opinions and attitudes. Of course you will want your opinions to be* your own. *Return the completed forms* promptly. *Use a pencil and make your markings as clear as possible.*

Part I—Some Facts About Yourself

(In all cases put an "X" in the box standing beside your answer. The printed numbers are to be ignored; they are for tabulation purposes.)

A. *CLASS IN COLLEGE*

Freshman .... ☐ 1
Sophomore .... ☐ 2
Junior .... ☐ 3
Senior .... ☐ 4

B. *AGE*

16 .... ☐ 1   21 .... ☐ 6
17 .... ☐ 2   22 .... ☐ 7
18 .... ☐ 3   23 .... ☐ 8
19 .... ☐ 4   24 .... ☐ 9
20 .... ☐ 5   25 .... ☐ 0
                        Over 25 .... ☐ Y

C. *MARITAL STATUS*

Single .... ☐ 1
Married .... ☐ 2
Widowed, Divorced, Separated .... ☐ 3

D. *SEX*

Male .... ☐ 1
Female .... ☐ 2

E. *MAJOR FIELD*

Arts (Humanities) .... ☐ 1
Social sciences .... ☐ 2
Science .... ☐ 3
Home Economics .... ☐ 4
Pre-engineering .... ☐ 5
Undecided .... ☐ 6

F. *VETERAN STATUS*

Veteran .... ☐ 1
Non-veteran .... ☐ 2

G. What is your approximate all-college grade average?

A .... ☐ 1   C+ .... ☐ 6
A— .... ☐ 2   C .... ☐ 7
B+ .... ☐ 3   C— .... ☐ 8
B .... ☐ 4   D+ .... ☐ 9
B— .... ☐ 5   D .... ☐ 0
                      D— .... ☐ Y

H. Are you currently employed (for remuneration) 16 hrs. per week or more?

Yes .... ☐ 1
No .... ☐ 2

I. Have you ever had full-time employment for one year or more? (excluding military service)

Yes .... ☐ 1
No .... ☐ 2

J. In how many extra-curricular activities or organizations are you active?

None .... ☐ 0   Four .... ☐ 4
One .... ☐ 1   Five .... ☐ 5
Two .... ☐ 2   Six or more .... ☐ 6
Three .... ☐ 3

PART II—Some General Attitudes and Opinions
(Put "X" in box to indicate your opinion)

1. Which one of the following comes closest to being your MOST important reason for coming to college?

To get necessary background for continuing studies in a graduate or professional school .... ☐ 1
To get necessary background for a vocation .... ☐ 2
To get a background to help you in dealing with other people .... ☐ 3
To get a general cultural background, mainly for personal satisfaction .... ☐ 4
That it is just a good thing to do—no specific reason ... ☐ 5
Other .... ☐ 6

2. Do you believe you would have come to college this year if you had been offered an interesting job at say $65 per week with a reasonable future?

Yes .... ☐ 1
No .... ☐ 2
Uncertain .... ☐ 3

3. Which one of these statements comes closest to your attitude toward required and elective courses?

There are too many required courses .... ☐ 1
There is a good balance between required and elective courses .... ☐ 2
There are not enough required courses .... ☐ 3
Uncertain .... ☐ 4

4. Which one of these statements best describes your attitude toward your program in your major field?

I feel that I have to specialize too much within my major field .... ☐ 1

I feel that I can't specialize enough—too many required courses outside my field .... ☐ 2

I feel that there is a good balance between my general education and my specialization .... ☐ 3

Uncertain .... ☐ 4

5. Two instructors have different approaches to teaching. Read their approaches, then answer 5a, 5b, and 5c.

1. The first places emphasis on factual materials.
2. The second places emphasis on ideas.

Which instructor would you prefer for a course dealing with:

	First	Second
5a. The arts?	☐ 1	☐ 2
5b. The physical and biological sciences? ..	☐ 1	☐ 2
5c. The social sciences?	☐ 1	☐ 2

6. Two instructors differ in their personal participation in the course material. Read how they differ then answer 6a, 6b, and 6c.

1. The first makes classroom expression of personal opinions, convictions, value judgments, etc.
2. The second gives no evidence in classroom of personal opinions, value judgments, etc.

Which instructor would you prefer for a course dealing with:

	First	Second
6a. The arts?	☐ 1	☐ 2
6b. The physical and biological sciences?.....	☐ 1	☐ 2
6c. The social sciences?	☐ 1	☐ 2

7. Here is a list of qualities important to good teaching. Read the list carefully, then answer questions 7a, 7b, and 7c.

    1. Systematic organization of subject matter.
    2. Good speaking ability.
    3. Ability to explain clearly.
    4. Ability to encourage thought.
    5. Sympathetic attitude toward students.
    6. Expert knowledge of subject.
    7. Enthusiastic attitude toward subject.
    8. Fairness in making and grading tests.
    9. Tolerance toward student disagreement.
    10. Pleasing personality.

7a. Of the above qualities, which *three* would you consider to be of greatest importance in a course dealing with the physical and biological sciences?
(Put an "X" in *three* boxes corresponding to qualities you select.)

☐ ☐ ☐ ☐ ☐ ☐ ☐ ☐ ☐ ☐
1 2 3 4 5 6 7 8 9 10

7b. Of these qualities, which *three* would you consider to be of greatest importance in a course dealing with the social sciences—history, economics, sociology, etc.
(Put an "X" in *three* boxes corresponding to qualities you select.)

☐ ☐ ☐ ☐ ☐ ☐ ☐ ☐ ☐ ☐
1 2 3 4 5 6 7 8 9 10

7c. Which *three* would you consider of greatest importance in a course dealing with the arts—literature, languages, fine arts, etc.
(Put an "X" in *three* boxes corresponding to qualities you select.)

☐ ☐ ☐ ☐ ☐ ☐ ☐ ☐ ☐ ☐
1 2 3 4 5 6 7 8 9 10

PART III—Rating the Qualifications of an Instructor

On the next page of this form you are asked to rate one of your instructors. For purposes of analyzing the survey results, we wish you to rate one certain instructor on *this* form. (You will have a chance to rate the others on the white form.)

HOW TO DETERMINE WHICH INSTRUCTOR TO RATE ON THIS FORM

A. Think of the *order* in which you meet your different instructors during the week. Thus your first class contact might be Monday at 9, your second on Monday at 11, your third on Tuesday at 10 and so on. In this way you can determine which instructor you meet first, second, third, fourth, and fifth each week.

B. *If your last name begins with a letter between:*   *Rate on this form the instructor you meet:*

    A–E .... FIRST
    F–H .... SECOND
    I–L .... THIRD
    M–R .... FOURTH
    S–Z .... FIFTH

C. NAME OF INSTRUCTOR .... DEPARTMENT ....

D. Now look up this instructor on the printed list. Beside his name is a code number. Write the instructor's code number in this box .... ☐

Now that the instructor to rate on this form has been determined, please answer these questions about the course that you have with him at that hour.

E. Is there more than one instructor regularly teaching you in this course?

Yes .... ☐

No .... ☐ 1

IF "YES": Does the instructor you are rating teach in a:

Lecture .... ☐ 2

Laboratory .... ☐ 3

Recitation .... ☐ 4

F. Are you taking the course as a required or as an elective course?

Required .... ☐ 1

Elective .... ☐ 2

G. Is the catalog number of this course:

10 or under .... ☐ 1

Above 10 .... ☐ 2

H. Approximately how many students are there in the class?

1–9 .... ☐ 1

10–19 .... ☐ 2

20–29 .... ☐ 3

30–39 .... ☐ 4

40–49 .... ☐ 5

50 or more .... ☐ 6

I. Make as close an approximation as you can to your grade standing in this course.

A	☐ 1	C+	☐ 6
A—	☐ 2	C	☐ 7
B+	☐ 3	C—	☐ 8
B	☐ 4	D+	☐ 9
B—	☐ 5	D	☐ 0
		Below D	☐ Y
		No estimate possible	☐ X

READ: Here is a list of ten qualities important to good teaching, each divided into a scale. Read each category carefully and decide how you would rate your instructor on the individual quality. If you have difficulty reaching a decision, select the answer that comes closest to how you feel about the instructor.

Place an "X" in *one* of the boxes under each of the ten categories.

1. *ORGANIZATION OF SUBJECT MATTER*

Systematic and thoroughly organized .... ☐ 1
Adequate, could be better .... ☐ 2
Inadequate organization detracts from course .... ☐ 3
Confused and unsystematic .... ☐ 4
                                                    X

---

2. *SPEAKING ABILITY*

Skilled in presenting material, voice and presence
excellent .... ☐ 5
Adequate, does not detract from course .... ☐ 6
Poor speaker, detracts from course .... ☐ 7
Poor speaking techniques serious handicap in course .. ☐ 8
                                                    Y

---

3. *ABILITY TO EXPLAIN*

Explanations clear and to point .... ☐ 1
Explanations usually adequate .... ☐ 2
Explanations often inadequate .... ☐ 3
Explanations seldom given or usually inadequate .... ☐ 4
                                                    X

---

4. *ENCOURAGEMENT TO THINKING*

Has great ability to make you think for yourself ...... ☐ 5
Considerable stimulation to thinking .... ☐ 6
Not much stimulus to thinking .... ☐ 7
Discouraging to thought .... ☐ 8
                                                    Y

5. ATTITUDE TOWARD STUDENTS

Sympathetic, helpful, actively concerned .... ☐ 1
Moderately sympathetic .... ☐ 2
Routine in attitude—avoids individual contact .... ☐ 3
Distant, aloof, cold .... ☐ 4
X

6. KNOWLEDGE OF SUBJECT

Exceedingly well informed in field of course .... ☐ 5
Adequately informed .... ☐ 6
Not well informed .... ☐ 7
Very inadequately informed .... ☐ 8
Y

7. ATTITUDE TOWARD SUBJECT

Enthusiastic, enjoys teaching .... ☐ 1
Rather interested .... ☐ 2
Rather bored—routine interest .... ☐ 3
Not interested, disillusioned with subject .... ☐ 4
X

8. FAIRNESS IN EXAMINATIONS

Testing excellently done .... ☐ 5
Testing is satisfactory .... ☐ 6
Testing sometimes unfair .... ☐ 7
Testing mostly unfair .... ☐ 8
Y

9. TOLERANCE TO DISAGREEMENT

Encourages and values reasonable disagreement ...... ☐ 1
Accepts disagreement fairly well .... ☐ 2
Discourages disagreement .... ☐ 3
Dogmatic, intolerant of disagreement .... ☐ 4
X

10. *INSTRUCTOR AS "HUMAN BEING"*

Attractive personality, would like to know him ...... ☐ 5
Satisfactory personality .... ☐ 6
Rather unattractive personality .... ☐ 7
Not the kind of person you care for .... ☐ 8
Y

---

11. Of the ten italicized categories above, which *one* would you say represents the greatest weakness of the instructor you have rated?

(Put an "X" in the box corresponding to the number of the category you select.)

☐ ☐ ☐ ☐ ☐ ☐ ☐ ☐ ☐ ☐
1 2 3 4 5 6 7 8 9 10

---

12. Which *one* of the italicized categories would you say represents his strongest asset?

(Put an "X" in the box corresponding to the number of the category you select.)

☐ ☐ ☐ ☐ ☐ ☐ ☐ ☐ ☐ ☐
1 2 3 4 5 6 7 8 9 10

---

13. Compared to all college instructors you have had, how would you rate this instructor as a teacher?

Excellent.. ☐ 1   Good.. ☐ 2   Fair.. ☐ 3   Poor.. ☐ 4